Tried & True

13 Classic Quilts for Reproduction Fabrics

Jo Morton

Martingale
Create with Confidence

Tried & True: 13 Classic Quilts for Reproduction Fabrics

Martingale®
19021 120th Ave. NE, Ste. 102
Bothell, WA 98011-9511 USA
ShopMartingale.com

Printed in Hong Kong
25 24 23 22 21 20 8 7 6 5 4 3 2 1

Library of Congress Cataloging-in-Publication Data is available upon request.

ISBN: 978-1-68356-075-3

MISSION STATEMENT

We empower makers who use fabric and yarn to make life more enjoyable.

CREDITS

PUBLISHER AND CHIEF VISIONARY OFFICER
Jennifer Erbe Keltner

CONTENT DIRECTOR
Karen Costello Soltys

MANAGING EDITOR
Tina Cook

ACQUISITIONS AND DEVELOPMENT EDITOR
Laurie Baker

COPY EDITOR
Durby Peterson

DESIGN MANAGER
Adrienne Smitke

PRODUCTION MANAGER
Regina Girard

COVER AND BOOK DESIGNER
Kathy Kotomaimoce

LOCATION PHOTOGRAPHER
Adam Albright

STUDIO PHOTOGRAPHER
Brent Kane

ILLUSTRATOR
Sandy Loi

SPECIAL THANKS
Photography for this book was taken at Carol Hansen's Garden Barn in Indianola, Iowa.

Contents

Introduction

Making new quilts that have vintage appeal has been my quiltmaking journey since 1980. The colors used in antique quilts, and sometimes their design quirks, are what hooked me on making quilts back then, and they still keep me loving the look of quilts from the past. And because my husband, Russ, and I live in a 90-year-old home that I've filled with antiques and excellent reproductions, it all works for me.

If you're familiar with my work, you've probably noticed that I like to make small quilts. But, I do occasionally make larger wall-hanging and lap-sized quilts, which are what you'll find in this book. I like to use my quilts, and sometimes I need a larger quilt to fit a particular place on a wall or to drape over a cupboard door or the back of the couch. Plus, who doesn't enjoy wrapping up in a quilt on a brisk day? We get plenty of snuggle-worthy weather where I live in the Midwest, so it's always nice to grab a quilt and take the chill off.

To help you on your quiltmaking journey, throughout this book I've scattered tips for constructing the quilts and included tips on fabric choices in the projects. Most of the quilts are scrappy, just like the antique ones that inspired them, and with thoughtful placement of colors and prints you can make your quilts sparkle. You'll find additional helpful information, including my back-basting appliqué method and my clipping trick for reducing bulk, in "Jo's Favorite Techniques" on page 91.

I'm so glad to have you stitching some of my favorite quilt patterns. Making quilts is fun, but quilting with others who understand the need to create is nothing short of pure joy!

~Jo

Picnic Time

Churn Dash blocks never go out of style! The blocks in this quilt were from a block exchange with a patriotic theme. But with its soft Americana look, this timeless quilt can be enjoyed all year long—for picnics celebrated in the great outdoors as well as for ones held inside by the fireplace.

Finished Quilt: 51⅝" × 51⅝" **Finished Block:** 5⅝" × 5⅝"

Materials

Yardage is based on 42"-wide fabric. Fat quarters are 18" × 21".

- 24 rectangles, at least 4" × 8", of assorted shirting and toast prints for blocks (collectively referred to as *shirting)*
- 24 rectangles, at least 4" × 8", of assorted red and blue prints for blocks (collectively referred to as *dark)*
- ⅝ yard of red stripe for blocks
- ½ yard of cream-and-blue print for pieced inner border
- ½ yard of medium blue print for pieced inner border
- ⅞ yard of cream print for setting squares
- 1⅜ yards of red floral for outer border*
- 1 fat quarter of dark blue print for outer-border corners
- ¼ yard of medium blue stripe for single-fold binding
- 3½ yards of fabric for backing
- 58" × 58" square of batting

**Cut border strips along the lengthwise grain because it has less stretch. If you want to cut crosswise strips, you'll need only ¾ yard.*

Cutting

All measurements include ¼" seam allowances.

Cutting for 1 Block

Cut 24 total. Because the red stripe is used in each block, cutting instructions also include the total number of pieces if you want to cut them all at once.

From the shirting, cut *along the lengthwise grain*:

2 squares, 2½" × 2½"
1 strip, 1¼" × 7"
1 square, 1½" × 1½"

From the dark print, cut *along the lengthwise grain*:

2 squares, 2½" × 2½"
1 strip, 1¼" × 7"

From the red stripe, cut:

2 squares (48 total), 3¾" × 3¾"; cut in half diagonally to yield 4 triangles (96 total)

Cutting for Setting, Border, and Binding

From the cream-and-blue print, cut:

11 squares, 6" × 6"
2 squares, 2⅜" × 2⅜"

From the medium blue print, cut:

11 squares, 6" × 6"
2 squares, 2⅜" × 2⅜"

Continued on page 8

Continued from page 7

From the cream print, cut:
25 squares, 6⅛" × 6⅛"

From the red floral, cut *along the lengthwise grain*:
4 strips, 4½" × 43⅝"

From the dark blue print, cut:
4 squares, 4½" × 4½"

From the medium blue stripe, cut:
6 strips, 1⅛" × 42"

Making the Blocks

Use a scant ¼" seam allowance. Press all seam allowances as shown by the arrows in the illustrations.

1 Select one set of block pieces. Draw a diagonal line from corner to corner on the wrong side of the two shirting 2½" squares. Layer each marked square right sides together with a dark 2½" square. Sew a scant ¼" from both sides of the drawn line. Cut the layered squares apart on the marked lines to make four half-square-triangle units. Trim the units to measure 2" square.

Make 4 units.

2 Join the shirting and dark 1¼" × 7" strips along the long edges to make a strip set. Crosscut the strip set into four segments, 1½" wide.

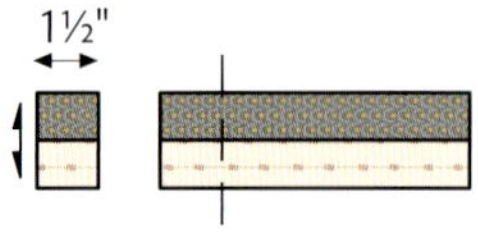

Make 1 strip set, 2" × 7".
Cut 4 segments, 1½" × 2".

3 Lay out the half-square-triangle units, the strip-set segments, and the shirting 1½" square in three horizontal rows as shown. Sew the pieces in each row together. Sew the rows together, matching seam intersections. Refer to "Clipping Trick" on page 92 to clip the seam intersections. Press the seam allowances toward the middle row and press the clipped intersections open. The churn dash unit should measure 4½" square, including seam allowances.

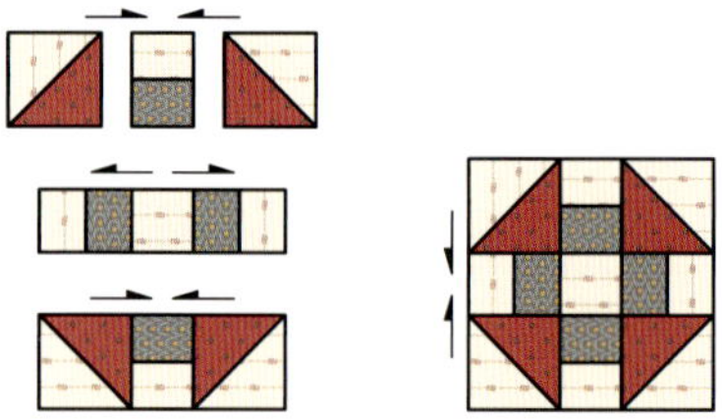
Make 1 unit,
4½" × 4½".

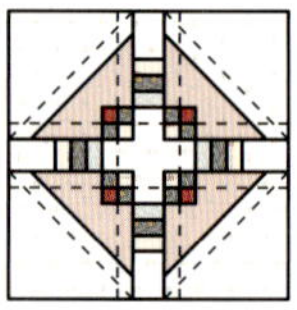
Pressing plan

4 Sew red stripe triangles to opposite sides of the churn dash unit. Repeat on the remaining two sides of the unit. Trim the block to measure 6⅛" square. Make a total of 24 blocks.

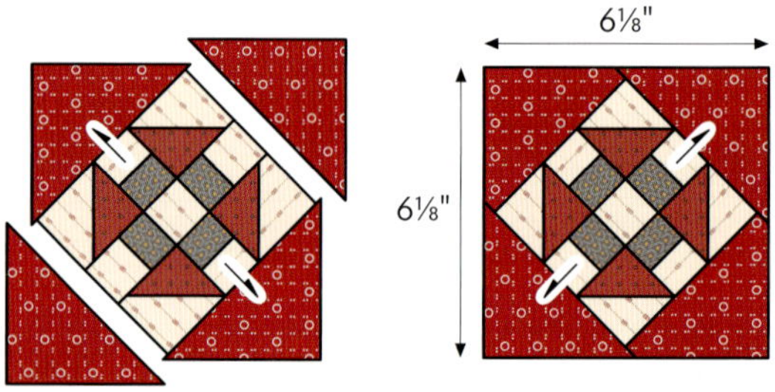

Make 24 blocks.

Making the Inner-Border Strips

1 Draw a diagonal line from corner to corner to form an X on the wrong side of each cream-and-blue 6" square.

2 Layer a marked square right sides together with a medium blue 6" square. Sew a scant ¼" from both sides of the drawn lines.

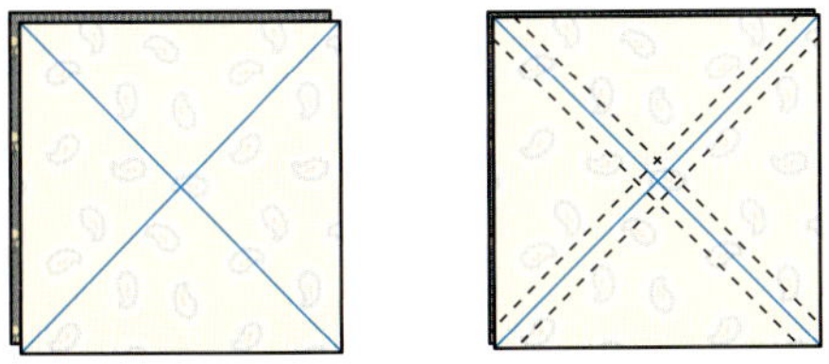

3 Cut the layered squares in half horizontally and vertically first, and then cut the individual units apart on the marked lines to make eight half-square-triangle units. Trim each unit to measure 2⅜" square.

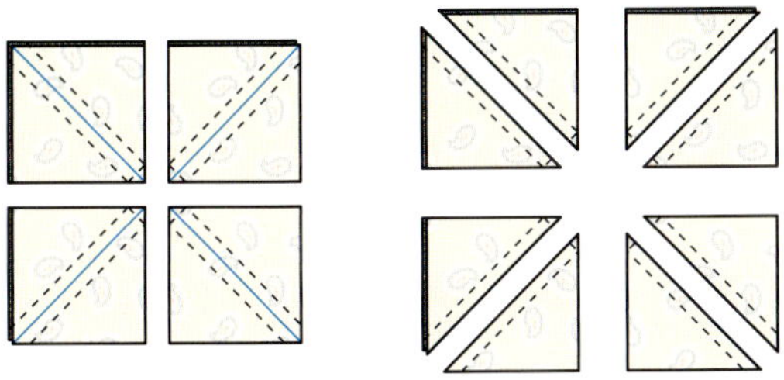

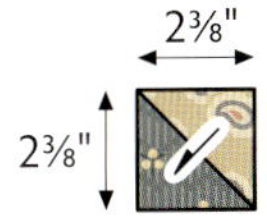

Make 8 units.

4 Repeat steps 2 and 3 to make a total of 88 half-square-triangle units. (You only need 84, so 4 will be extra.)

5 Referring to the diagram on page 11, arrange 21 half-square-triangle units for the top border, noting the position of the blue triangles. Sew the units together in pairs, and then sew the pairs together. The border strip should measure 2⅜" × 39⅞", including seam allowances. Repeat to make the bottom border strip. In the same manner and noting the position of the blue triangles, join 21 half-square triangles to make a side border strip. Add a medium blue and a

By ***Jo Morton;*** *machine quilted by* ***Maggi Honeyman***

cream-and-blue 2⅜" square to the ends of the strip. Repeat to make a total of two side border strips measuring 2⅜" × 43⅝", including seam allowances.

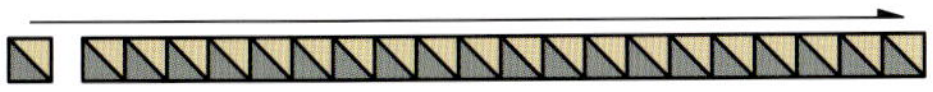

Make 2 top/bottom borders, 2⅜" × 39⅞".

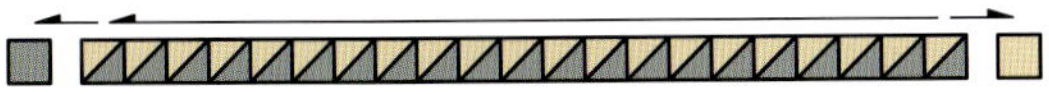

Make 2 side borders, 2⅜" × 43⅝".

Assembling the Quilt Top

1 Referring to the quilt assembly diagram, arrange the Churn Dash blocks and cream 6⅛" square setting blocks in seven rows of seven blocks each, alternating the blocks in each row and from row to row. Divide the blocks into quadrants as shown. Sew the blocks in each quadrant together into rows. Pin and sew the rows of each quadrant together, matching seam intersections. Clip the seam intersections. Press the seam allowances toward the setting blocks and press the clipped intersections open.

SEWING IN QUADRANTS

I am not a fan of piecing long rows and then sewing those long rows together. I sew blocks into four quadrants; usually the quadrants are not all equal, due to an odd number of horizontal and vertical rows. The four smaller sections are easier to sew, press, and handle. Then I have only one long seam to sew until adding the borders. I use my clipping trick at *all* of the seam intersections.

2 Pin and sew the quadrants together, clipping and pressing as before. The quilt center should measure 39⅞" square, including seam allowances.

Quilt assembly

3 Referring to the adding borders diagram below, pin and sew the pieced top and bottom border strips to the top and bottom of the quilt. Pin and sew the pieced side border strips to the sides of the quilt, matching seam intersections. Clip the seam intersections. Press the seam allowances toward the quilt center and press the clipped intersections open. The quilt top should measure 43⅝" square, including seam allowances.

4 Pin and sew two red floral 4½" × 43⅝" outer-border strips to the sides of the quilt. Sew the dark blue 4½" squares to the ends of the remaining red floral strips. Join these strips to the top and bottom of the quilt, matching seam intersections. Clip the seam intersections. Press the seam allowances toward the outer border and press the clipped intersections open. The quilt top should measure 51⅝" square.

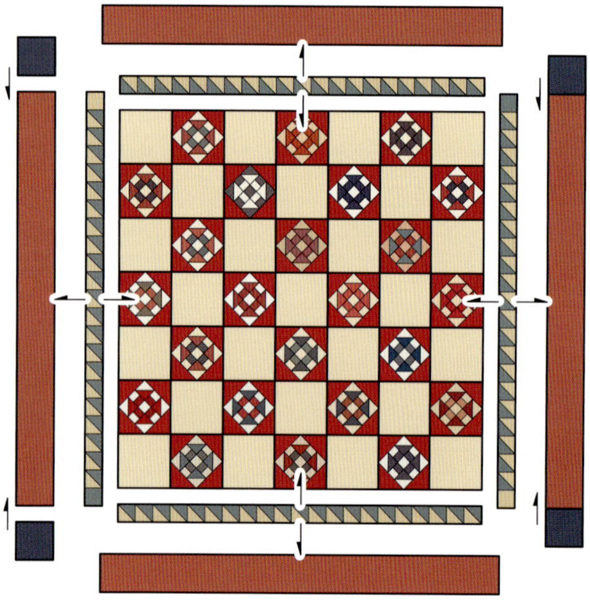

Adding borders

Quilting and Finishing

For more information about any finishing steps, visit ShopMartingale.com/HowtoQuilt.

1 Layer the quilt top, batting, and backing. Baste the layers together.

2 Hand or machine quilt as desired. In the quilt shown, the blocks are machine quilted in the ditch; a crosshatch design is quilted in the red corners of the blocks, with lines spaced about 1" apart. The setting blocks are quilted ¼" in from the seams to form a frame that is filled with a beautiful square feather wreath. The inner and outer borders are quilted as one in a crosshatch design, with the spacing established by the diagonal line of the inner-border units.

3 Use the medium blue stripe 1⅛"-wide strips to make single-fold binding; attach the binding to the quilt. For more detailed information about my technique for making the binding and attaching it, see "Single-Fold Binding" on page 94.

Union

Similar to a traditional Union block, this block design has a narrower outer round. I first noticed the design in several antique quilt blocks I purchased in Houston and thought it would be perfect for a block exchange. It seems that the person in charge (me) miscalculated the number of blocks needed, so we all ended up with enough blocks for two quilts!

Finished Quilt: 62" × 72" **Finished Block:** 7" × 7"

Materials

Yardage is based on 42"-wide fabric.

- 30 rectangles, 8" × 10", of assorted shirting prints for blocks
- 30 rectangles, 6" × 9", of assorted dark prints for blocks
- 30 rectangles, 4" × 7½", of assorted medium prints for blocks
- 1¼ yards of brown print #1 for setting squares and single-fold binding
- 1 yard of red print for setting triangles
- 2¼ yards of brown print #2 for border
- 3⅞ yards of fabric for backing
- 68" × 78" piece of batting
- 1" finished triangle papers (optional; see "Paper-Piecing Triangles" on page 16)

FABRIC CHOICES

I used one dark, one medium, and one shirting print in most of the blocks, but there are several variations to the basic color scheme used in this quilt. For some blocks, I used the dark print in place of the medium print. In other blocks, I used the medium print for the half-square-triangle units rather than the dark print. Look closely and you'll see a couple of other variations too. Variety is the spice that puts flavor in your quilts!

Cutting

All measurements include ¼" seam allowances.

Cutting for 1 Block

You'll need a total of 30 blocks, but it's easier to cut them one at a time.

From a shirting print, cut:
- 2 squares, 2¾" × 2¾"; cut in half diagonally to yield 4 triangles
- 6 squares, 2" × 2"
- 4 rectangles, 1½" × 3½"

From a dark print, cut:
- 1 square, 3" × 3"
- 6 squares, 2" × 2"

From a medium print, cut:
- 2 squares, 3½" × 3½"; cut in half diagonally to yield 4 triangles

Cutting for Setting, Border, and Binding

From brown print #1, cut:
- 4 strips, 7½" × 42"; crosscut into 20 squares, 7½" × 7½"
- 7 strips, 1⅛" × 42"

From the red print, cut:
- 2 strips, 12" × 42"; crosscut into 5 squares, 12" × 12". Cut each square into quarters diagonally to yield 20 side setting triangles (2 are extra).
- 2 squares, 6½" × 6½"; cut in half diagonally to yield 4 corner setting triangles

From brown print #2, cut *along the lengthwise grain*:
- 2 strips, 6½" × 72"
- 2 strips, 6½" × 60"

Making the Blocks

Use a scant ¼" seam allowance. Press all seam allowances as shown by the arrows in the illustrations.

1 Select one set of block pieces. Sew two shirting triangles to opposite sides of a dark 3" square. Sew the remaining two shirting triangles to the remaining sides of the square.

2 Trim the step 1 unit by aligning the 2" line of the ruler with the points of the center square. Trim one side and then rotate the block to cut the remaining sides. The trimmed unit should measure 4" square, including seam allowances.

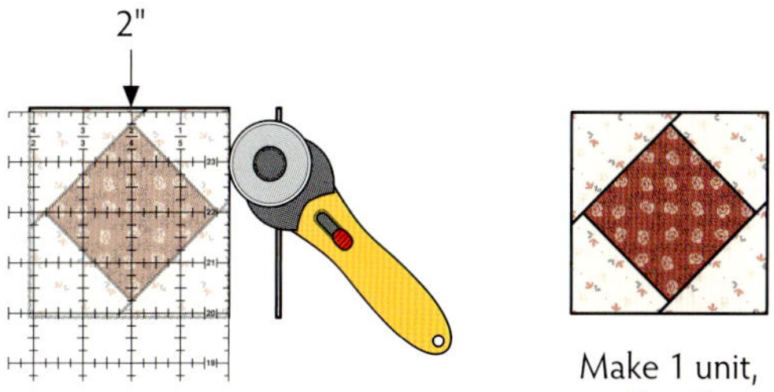

Make 1 unit, 4" × 4".

3 Sew two medium triangles to opposite sides of the unit from step 2. Sew the remaining two medium triangles to the remaining sides of the unit. Trim the unit to 5½" square as you did in step 2, placing the 2¾" line of the ruler on the points of the shirting triangles.

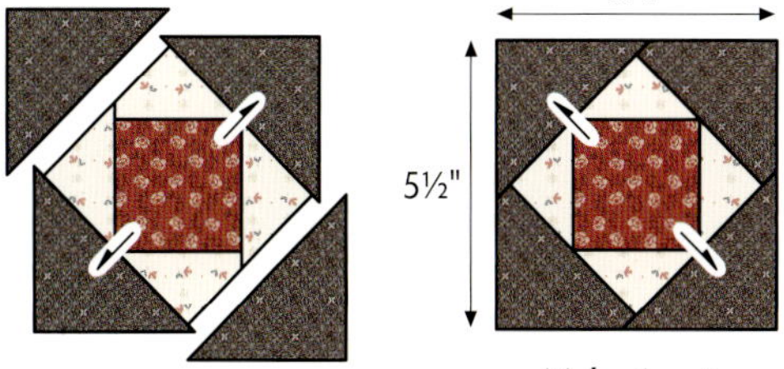

Make 1 unit.

Paper-Piecing Triangles

I recommend using triangle foundation paper for precision piecing when making the small half-square-triangle units. You'll need papers that yield 1" finished-size units, such as Star Singles or Triangle Papers by Primitive Gatherings. For this quilt, you'll need to make a total of 12 half-square-triangle units per block.

1 Cut the fabrics as indicated on the package. You'll need one dark (or medium) and one light square of fabric per sheet.

2 Layer the fabric squares right sides together and place the small sheet of 1" triangle paper on top of the light fabric. Sew as directed on the paper.

3 Cut the units apart, leaving the papers attached, and press seam allowances toward the darker fabric. Leaving the paper on the unit while pressing keeps the bias edge from bowing.

4 Remove the paper foundations. You can clip the corners of the half-square-triangle units and tear the papers away as you go, but I find that time consuming. I set the pressed units aside in a basket for later. I like to clip the corners and remove the papers while watching a favorite show on television.

4 Draw a diagonal line from corner to corner on the wrong side of each shirting 2" square. Layer a marked square with a dark 2" square, right sides together. Sew a scant ¼" from both sides of the drawn line. Cut the layered squares apart on the line to make two half-square-triangle units. Repeat to make a total of 12 units. Press and trim each unit to measure 1½" square.

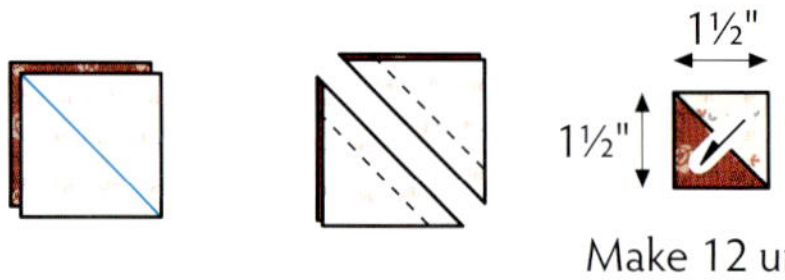

Make 12 units.

5 Join a half-square-triangle unit to the ends of each shirting 1½" × 3½" rectangle as shown. The pieced strips should measure 1½" × 5½", including seam allowances. Repeat to make a total of four pieced strips.

Make 4 pieced strips, 1½" × 5½".

6 Sew two pieced strips to opposite sides of the step 3 unit. Add a half-square-triangle unit to each end of the remaining two pieced strips. Join these strips to the remaining sides of the unit, matching seam intersections. Refer to "Clipping Trick" on page 92 to clip the seam intersections. Press the seam allowances toward the pieced strips and press the clipped intersections open. The block should measure 7½" square, including seam allowances.

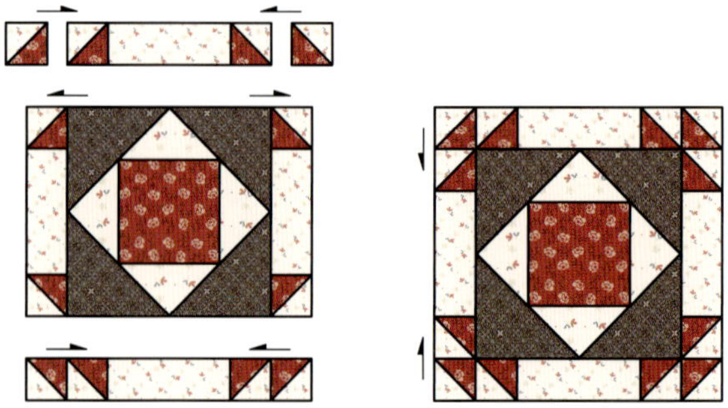
Make 1 block, 7½" × 7½".

7 Repeat steps 1–6 to make a total of 30 blocks.

By ***Jo Morton;*** *machine quilted by* ***Maggi Honeyman***

Assembling the Quilt Top

1 Refer to the quilt assembly diagram below to arrange the blocks and 7½" brown #1 setting squares into 10 diagonal rows. Rearrange the blocks until you're satisfied with the color placement. Add the red setting triangles to the edges and corners. Sew the blocks and setting pieces together in each row.

2 Pin and sew the rows together, matching seam intersections. Clip the seam intersections. Press the seam allowances toward the setting squares and triangles and press the clipped intersections open. Add the corner triangles last.

3 Trim the edges of the quilt ¼" from the block points. The quilt top should measure 50" × 60", including seam allowances.

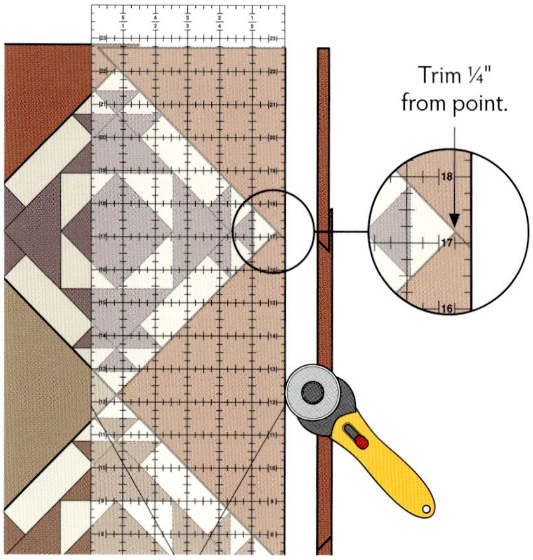

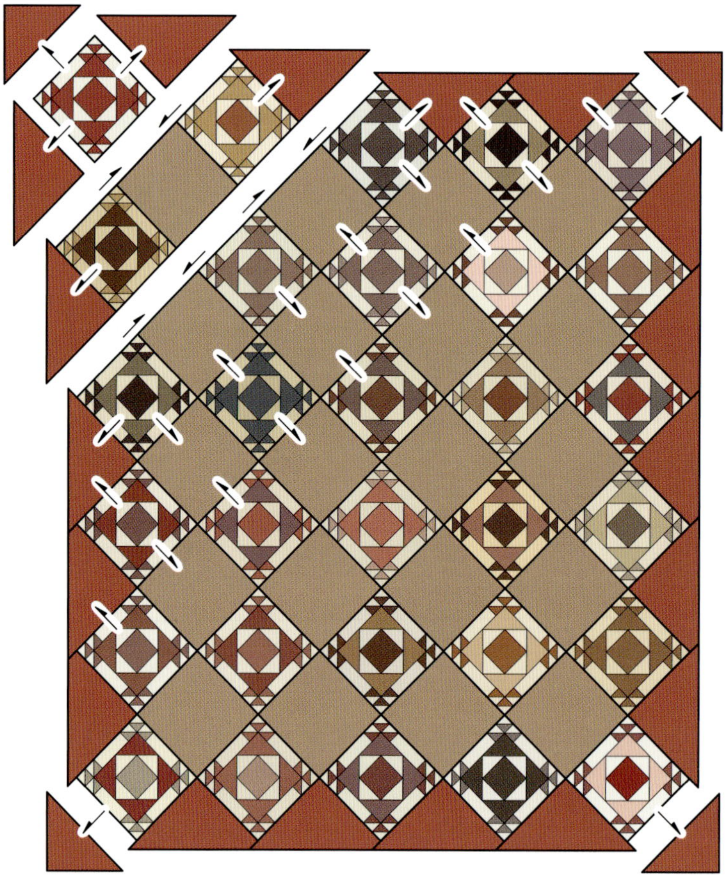

Quilt assembly

4 Pin and sew the 6½" × 60" brown #2 border strips to the sides of the quilt. Press the seam allowances toward the border strips. Pin and sew the 6½" × 72" brown #2 border strips to the top and bottom of the quilt. The quilt top should measure 62" × 72".

Quilting and Finishing

For more information about any finishing steps, visit ShopMartingale.com/HowtoQuilt.

1 Layer the quilt top, batting, and backing. Baste the layers together.

2 Hand or machine quilt as desired. The quilt shown is machine quilted in the ditch around each block, and each block center is quilted with a four-petal flower. The shirting and dark triangles are quilted ¼" inside their edges to repeat the triangle shape. The setting pieces and outer border all feature feather motifs.

3 Use the 1⅛"-wide brown #1 strips to make single-fold binding; attach the binding to the quilt. For more detailed information about my technique for making the binding and attaching it, see "Single-Fold Binding" on page 94.

Sing These Blues

While blue isn't my favorite color, it's quite lovely mixed with brown or rust. I wanted to showcase the blue striped fabric you see in the blocks, so an Album block seemed the perfect choice. To create an aged appearance, I overdyed some of the fabrics, including the medium blue print, with a tan dye—a trick that makes working with blues easier for me!

Finished Quilt: 36½" × 36½" **Finished Block:** 8" × 8"

Materials

Yardage is based on 42"-wide fabric.

- ½ yard *total* of assorted light brown, pink, and cream prints for blocks and outer border (collectively referred to as *light*)
- ⅔ yard *total* of assorted medium to dark brown and dark red prints for blocks and outer border (collectively referred to as *dark*)
- ½ yard of dark blue stripe for blocks
- 1⅛ yards of medium blue print for sashing and borders
- ¼ yard of dark red print for single-fold binding
- 1¼ yards of fabric for backing
- 43" × 43" square of batting

Cutting

All measurements include ¼" seam allowances.

Cutting for 1 Block

You'll need 9 blocks, but it's easier to cut scrappy blocks one at a time. Because the dark blue stripe is used in each block, cutting instructions also include the total number of pieces if you want to cut them all at once. Refer to the block assembly illustrations for the specific location of the A and B triangles, if needed.

From *1* light print, cut:
8 squares, 1⅞" × 1⅞"

From *1* dark print, cut:
2 squares, 3¼" × 3¼"; cut into quarters diagonally to yield 8 A triangles
1 rectangle, 1⅞" × 4¾"
2 squares, 1⅞" × 1⅞"

From the same or a different dark print, cut:
1 square, 3¼" × 3¼"; cut into quarters diagonally to yield 4 B triangles

From a different dark print, cut:
2 squares, 2" × 2"; cut in half diagonally to yield 4 corner triangles

From the dark blue stripe, fussy cut:
4 rectangles (36 total), 1⅞" × 4¾"

Continued on page 22

Continued from page 21

Cutting for Sashing, Borders, and Binding

From the medium blue print, cut along the *lengthwise* grain:

2 strips, 2½" × 32½"
4 strips, 2½" × 28½"
6 strips, 2½" × 8½"
34 squares, 3" × 3"

From the assorted light and dark prints, cut a *total* of:

34 squares, 3" × 3"

From the dark red print for binding, cut:

4 strips, 1⅛" × 42"

FABRIC CHOICES

The cutting instructions are for A triangles that match the center X fabric, but there are several different ways to use your fabrics when making these blocks. For some blocks, I used the same fabric for the B triangles, center X pieces, and A triangles. In other blocks, I used the same fabric for the B triangles and center X pieces but used a different fabric for the A triangles. This block is great for using up smaller scraps in your stash, so take advantage of what you have when selecting the fabrics for each position.

Making the Blocks

Use a scant ¼" seam allowance. Press all seam allowances as shown by the arrows in the illustrations.

1 Select one set of block pieces. Sew light 1⅞" squares to opposite sides of a dark 1⅞" square, using a very scant ¼" seam allowance. The pieced strip should measure 1⅞" × 4¾", including seam allowances, so you may need to adjust seam allowances to achieve the correct length. Repeat to make a total of two units. Join these units to the long edges of the dark 1⅞" × 4¾" rectangle. The center should measure 4¾" square, including seam allowances. Again, you may need to adjust the seam allowances to achieve the correct measurement.

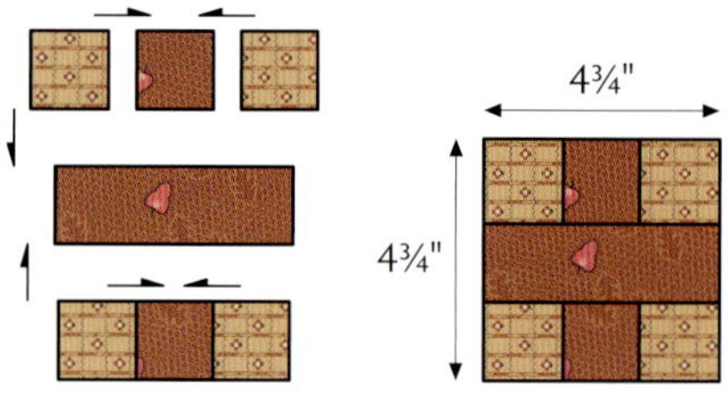

Make 1 unit.

2 Sew dark blue stripe 1⅞" × 4¾" rectangles to opposite sides of the center square. Join B triangles to the ends of two dark blue stripe 1⅞" × 4¾" rectangles. Sew these strips to the remaining sides of the center square.

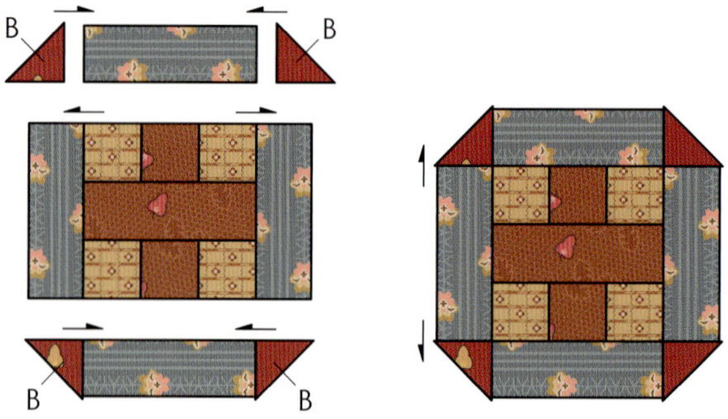

*By **Jo Morton**; machine quilted by **Debbie Roberts***

3 Join A triangles to opposite sides of a light 1⅞" square. Sew a corner triangle to the top of the unit. Repeat to make a total of four corner units.

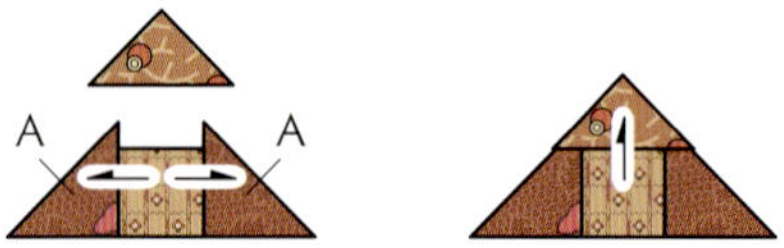

Make 4 corner units.

4 Sew corner units to opposite sides of a step 2 unit. Repeat on the remaining sides of the unit to complete the block. The block should measure 8½" square, including seam allowances. Make nine blocks total.

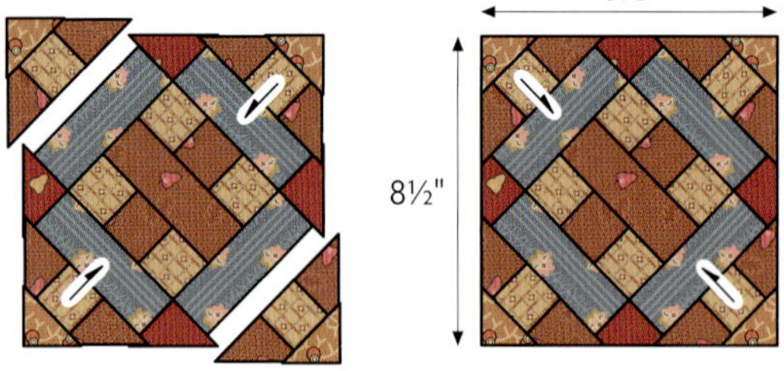

Make 9 blocks.

Assembling the Quilt Top

1 Refer to the quilt assembly diagram below to arrange the blocks and medium blue 2½" × 8½" vertical sashing strips in three rows of three blocks and two sashing strips each, alternating them as shown. Sew the pieces into rows. The rows should measure 8½" × 28½", including seam allowances.

2 Join the block rows and two medium blue 2½" × 28½" horizontal sashing strips, alternating them as shown and making sure to align the vertical sashing from row to row. The quilt center should measure 28½" square, including seam allowances.

3 Sew medium blue 2½" × 28½" inner-border strips to opposite sides of the quilt center. Join the medium blue 2½" × 32½" inner-border strips to the remaining sides of the quilt center. The quilt top should measure 32½" square, including seam allowances.

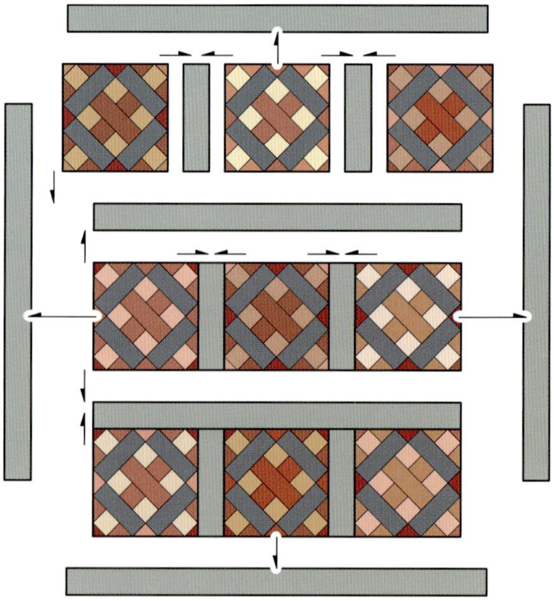

Quilt assembly

Adding the Sawtooth Outer Border

1 Draw a diagonal line from corner to corner on the wrong side of the 34 assorted print 3" squares.

2 Layer a marked square with a medium blue 3" square, right sides together. Sew a scant ¼" from both sides of the drawn line. Cut the layered squares apart on the line to make two half-square-triangle units. Press and trim the units to measure 2½" square. Repeat to make a total of 68 half-square-triangle units.

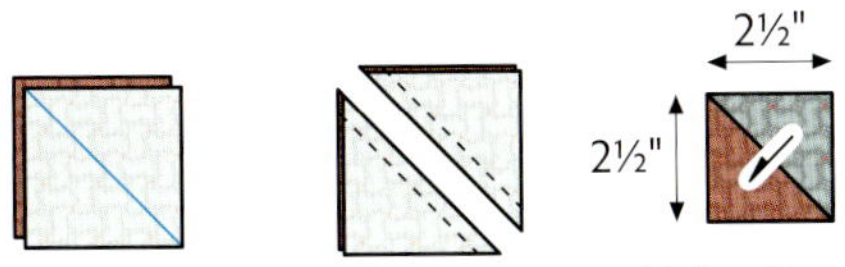

Make 68 units.

3 Arrange and sew 16 half-square-triangle units together as shown to make a sawtooth outer-border strip. Be careful when pressing so that you don't stretch the border. Repeat to make a total of three outer-border strips with the print triangles facing right and one with the print triangles facing left. All borders should measure 2½" × 32½", including seam allowances.

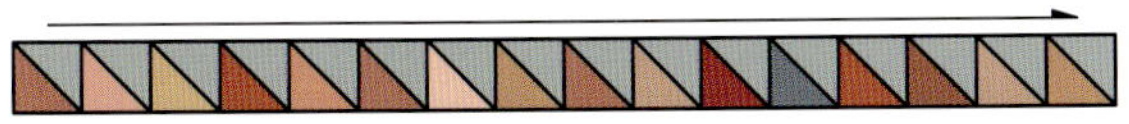
Make 3 borders, 2½" × 32½".

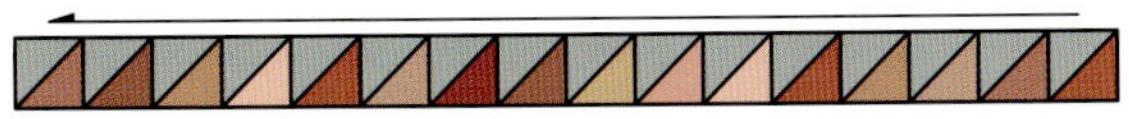
Make 1 left border, 2½" × 32½".

4 Pin and sew the left border to the left edge of the quilt. Pin and sew one of the remaining borders to the right edge of the quilt. Sew the remaining half-square-triangle units to the ends of the remaining sawtooth borders, noting the direction of the blue triangles. Pin and sew these borders to the remaining sides of the quilt. Refer to "Clipping Trick" on page 92 to clip the seam intersections. The quilt top should measure 36½" square.

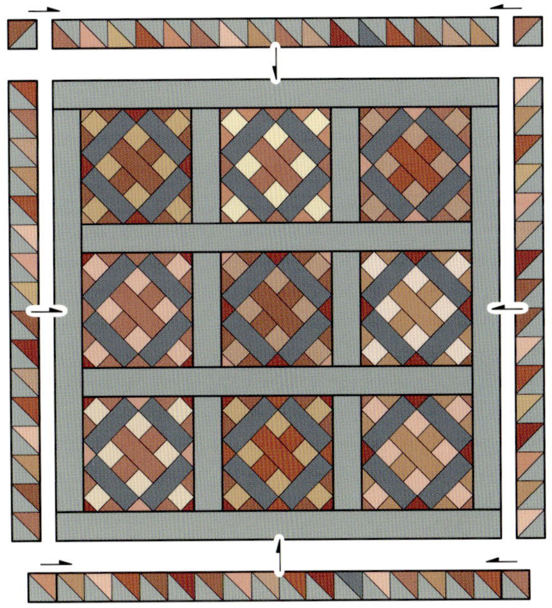
Adding the outer border

Quilting and Finishing

For more information about any finishing steps, visit ShopMartingale.com/HowtoQuilt.

1 Layer the quilt top, batting, and backing. Baste the layers together.

2 Hand or machine quilt as desired. The quilt shown is machine quilted with a crosshatch grid determined by the block seamlines and also quilted halfway between the lines, because we like lots of quilting! The sashing is stipple quilted and the outer sawtooth border is quilted in the ditch.

3 Use the dark red 1⅛"-wide strips to make single-fold binding; attach the binding to the quilt. For more detailed information about my technique for making the binding and attaching it, see "Single-Fold Binding" on page 94.

Glad Tidings

When I see a quilt that I like—whether it's the whole quilt or a block, a setting, or even just the colors—I keep a picture of it in an "inspiration" file. Several of the antique quilts in my file feature green and gold blocks sashed with red fabric. (Can you guess where I got the idea for this Nine Patch quilt?) Even though I tried to pair the greens and golds so no two blocks were alike, matching blocks happened. But I still love this quilt.

Finished Quilt: 39½" × 44¾" **Finished Block:** 3¾" × 3¾"

Materials

Yardage is based on 42"-wide fabric. Fat quarters are 18" × 21".

- 9 fat quarters of assorted gold prints for blocks and pieced inner border
- 8 fat quarters of assorted green prints for blocks and pieced inner border
- ⅝ yard of red print #1 for setting squares and triangles
- 1¼ yards of red print #2 for outer border
- ¼ yard of gold print for single-fold binding
- 2½ yards of fabric for backing
- 46" × 51" piece of batting

Cutting

All measurements include ¼" seam allowances.

From *each* of the gold prints, cut:
15 squares, 1¾" × 1¾" (135 total)

From the remainder of *each of 3* of the gold prints, cut:
5 squares, 1¾" × 1¾" (15 total)

From the remainder of the gold prints, cut a *total* of:
10 squares, 5" × 5"
1 square, 2½" × 2½"

From *each* of the green prints, cut:
12 squares, 1¾" × 1¾" (96 total)

From the remainder of *each of 6* of the green prints, cut:
4 squares, 1¾" × 1¾" (24 total)

From the remainder of the green prints, cut a *total* of:
10 squares, 5" × 5"
1 square, 2½" × 2½"

From red print #1, cut:
3 strips, 4¼" × 42"; crosscut into:
20 squares, 4¼" × 4¼"
2 squares, 4" × 4"; cut in half diagonally to yield 4 corner setting triangles
1 strip, 6¾" × 42"; crosscut into 5 squares, 6¾" × 6¾". Cut each square into quarters diagonally to yield 20 side setting triangles (2 are extra).

Continued on page 28

Continued from page 27

From red print #2, cut *along the lengthwise grain*:
2 strips, 5¼" × 39½"
2 strips, 5¼" × 35¼"

From the gold print for binding, cut:
5 strips, 1⅛" × 42"

Making the Blocks

Use a scant ¼" seam allowance. Press all seam allowances as shown by the arrows in the illustrations.

Arrange five matching gold 1¾" squares and four matching green 1¾" squares into three horizontal rows, alternating the colors in each row. Sew the squares in each row together. Pin and sew the rows together, matching seam intersections. Refer to "Clipping Trick" on page 92 to clip the seam intersections. Press the seam allowances toward the green squares and press the clipped intersections open. The block should measure 4¼" square, including seam allowances. Repeat to make a total of 30 blocks.

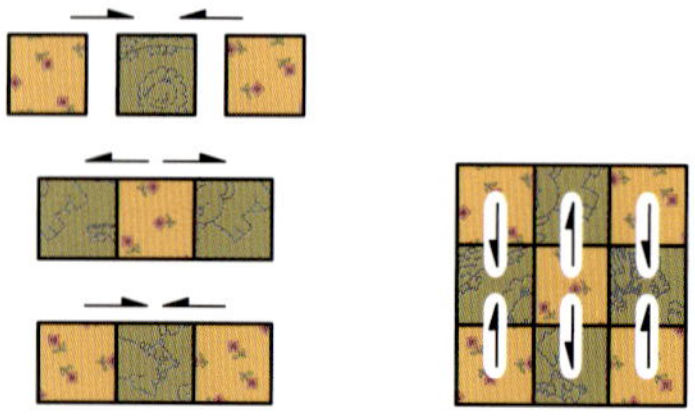

Make 30 blocks, 4¼" × 4¼".

Making the Inner-Border Strips

1 Draw a diagonal line from corner to corner in both directions on the wrong side of each gold 5" square, creating an X.

2 Layer a marked gold square right sides together with a green 5" square. Sew a scant ¼" from both sides of each line. Cut the layered squares in quarters horizontally and vertically, and then cut on the drawn lines to make eight half-square-triangle units. Carefully press each unit and trim to measure 2" square. Repeat to make a total of 80 half-square-triangle units.

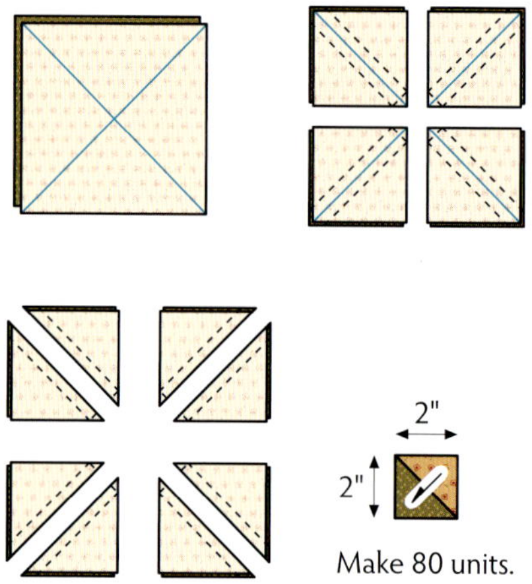

Make 80 units.

3 To make the additional two half-square-triangle units needed, draw a diagonal line from corner to corner on the wrong side of the gold 2½" square. Layer the marked square on top of the green 2½" square, right sides together. Sew a scant ¼" from each side of the drawn line. Cut the unit apart on the drawn line to make two half-square-triangle units. Trim each unit to measure 2" square. You'll now have a total of 82 half-square-triangle units.

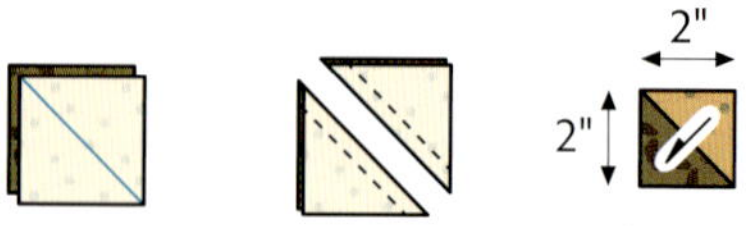

Make 2 units.

4 Arrange 21 half-square-triangle units as shown on page 29 for the side border strips and 20 half-square-triangle units for the top and bottom border strips, noting the direction of the gold triangles at the ends. Sew the units together in pairs, and then sew the pairs together. Make two of each border strip. In order for the strips to fit the quilt top, they'll need to measure 2" × 32¼"

and 2" × 30", including seam allowances. You may need to take in or let out a few seams to achieve the correct lengths.

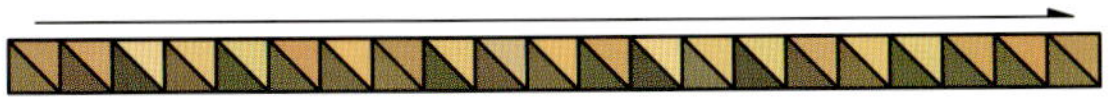

Make 2 side borders,
2" × 32¼".

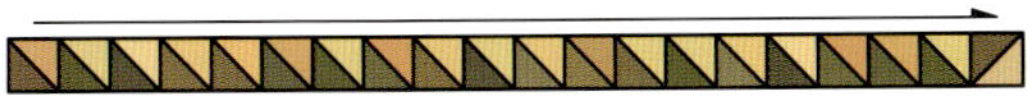

Make 2 top/bottom borders,
2" × 30".

Assembling the Quilt Top

1 Refer to the quilt assembly diagram below to arrange the blocks and 4¼" red #1 squares into 10 diagonal rows. Add the red #1 setting triangles to the edges and corners. Sew the blocks and setting pieces together in each row.

2 Pin and sew the rows together, matching seam intersections. Clip the seam intersections. Press the seam allowances toward the setting squares and triangles and press the clipped intersections open. Add the corner triangles last.

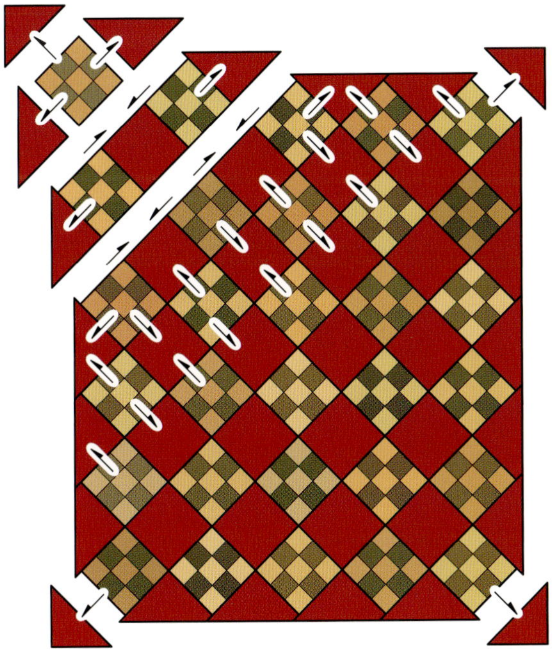

Quilt assembly

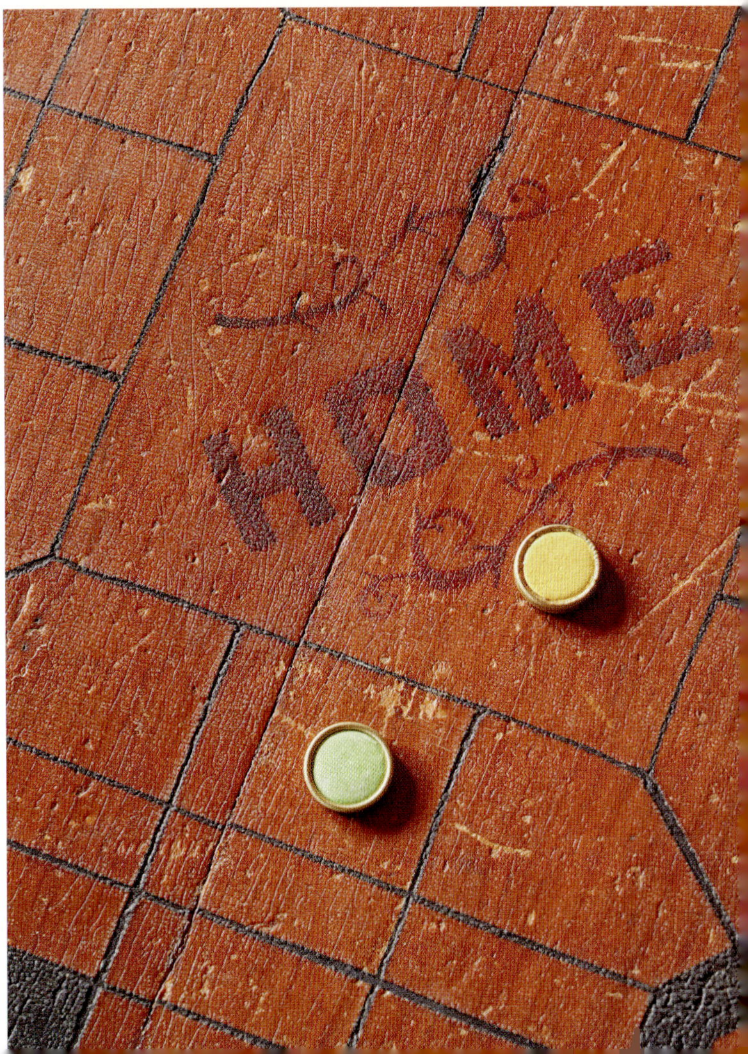

Designed by **Jo Morton**; *pieced by* **Jo Morton, Cindy Hansen, Mary Fornoff,** *and* **Phyllis Masters**; *machine quilted by* **Suzanne Earnest**

3 Trim the quilt top ¼" from the block points. The quilt top should measure 27" × 32¼", including seam allowances.

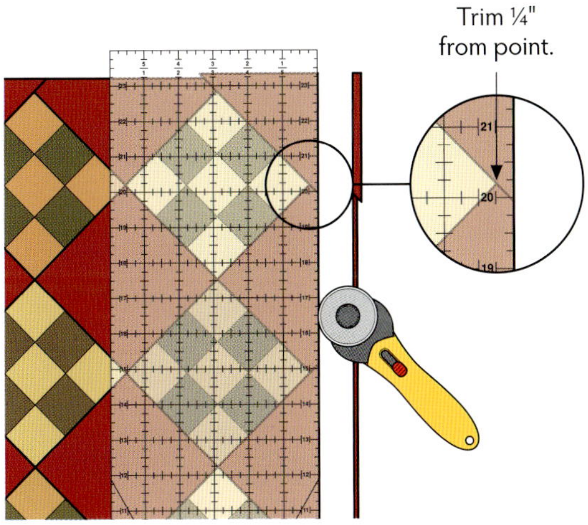

4 Pin and sew the 2" × 32¼" inner-border strips to the sides of the quilt. Pin and sew the 2" × 30" inner-border strips to the top and bottom of the quilt. The quilt top should measure 30" × 35¼", including seam allowances.

5 Sew the 5¼" × 35¼" red #2 outer-border strips to the sides of the quilt. Sew the 5¼" × 39½" red #2 outer-border strips to the top and bottom of the quilt. The quilt top should measure 39½" × 44¾".

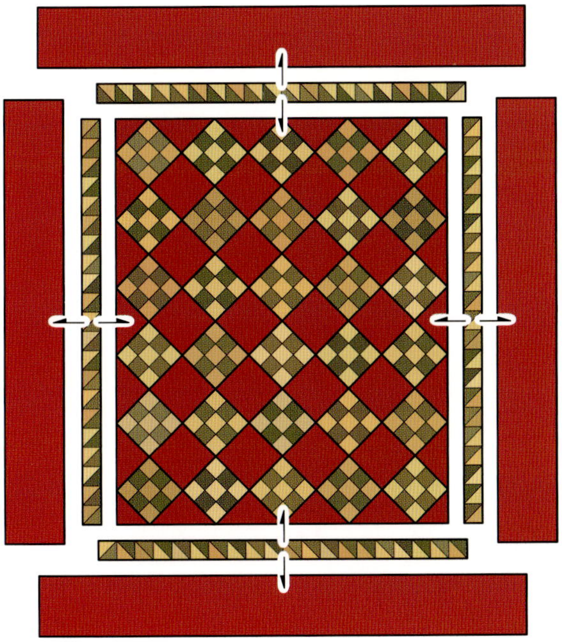

Adding borders

Quilting and Finishing

For more information about any finishing steps, visit ShopMartingale.com/HowtoQuilt.

1 Layer the quilt top, batting, and backing. Baste the layers together.

2 Hand or machine quilt as desired. The quilt shown is machine quilted in the ditch along the block edges. Each row of blocks is quilted with a straight line that extends from point to point through the horizontal and vertical centers. A square is stitched ⅞" inside the outer edges of each block. The setting pieces are quilted with a nine-patch grid established by the block seams. The inner border is quilted in the ditch, and the outer border features a crosshatch grid established by the inner border.

3 Use the gold 1⅛"-wide strips to make single-fold binding; attach the binding to the quilt. For more detailed information about my technique for making the binding and attaching it, see "Single-Fold Binding" on page 94.

Cut the Mustard

The term "cut the mustard" means to rise up to expectations, and boy did this quilt do just that. I was very pleased with the results when I used the mustard print for the setting pieces and inner border. The color really warms up the quilt and sets off the indigo prints nicely. Mustard is a color that's become popular again, so this quilt not only has vintage charm, it also has a splash of modernity.

Finished Quilt: 57¼" × 65¾" **Finished Block:** 6" × 6"

Materials

Yardage is based on 42"-wide fabric. Fat quarters are 18" × 21".

- ⅞ yard *total* of assorted light prints for blocks
- 1⅓ yards *total* of assorted indigo prints for blocks and pieced inner border
- 1⅔ yards of mustard print for setting pieces and pieced inner border
- 1¾ yards of indigo print #1 for outer border
- 1 fat quarter of indigo print #2 for outer-border cornerstones
- ⅓ yard of indigo print #3 for single-fold binding
- 3⅝ yards of fabric for backing
- 64" × 72" piece of batting

Cutting

All measurements include ¼" seam allowances.

Cutting for 1 Block

You'll need a total of 30 blocks, but it's easier to cut them one at a time.

From *1* light print, cut:
2 squares, 3¼" × 3¼"
1 square, 2½" × 2½"

From *1* of the assorted indigo prints, cut:
2 squares, 3¼" × 3¼"
4 squares, 2½" × 2½"

Cutting for Setting, Borders, and Binding

From the mustard print, cut:
5 squares, 10" × 10"; cut into quarters diagonally to yield 20 side setting triangles (2 are extra)
20 squares, 6½" × 6½"
2 squares, 5¼" × 5¼"; cut in half diagonally to yield 4 corner setting triangles
2 squares, 3¼" × 3¼"
44 squares, 3" × 3"

From the assorted indigo prints, cut a *total* of:
11 squares, 5½" × 5½"
2 squares, 3¼" × 3¼"

From indigo print #1, cut *along the lengthwise grain*:
2 strips, 5½" × 55¾"
2 strips, 5½" × 47¼"

From indigo print #2, cut:
4 squares, 5½" × 5½"

From indigo print #3, cut:
7 strips, 1⅛" × 42"

Making the Blocks

Use a scant ¼" seam allowance. Press all seam allowances as shown by the arrows.

1 Select one set of block pieces. Draw a diagonal line from corner to corner in both directions on the wrong side of each light 3¼" square, creating an X. Layer each marked square right sides together with an indigo 3¼" square. Sew a scant ¼" from both sides of *one* drawn line on each layered pair. Cut the units apart on the drawn line between the stitching lines to make four half-square-triangle units measuring 2⅞" square, including seam allowances.

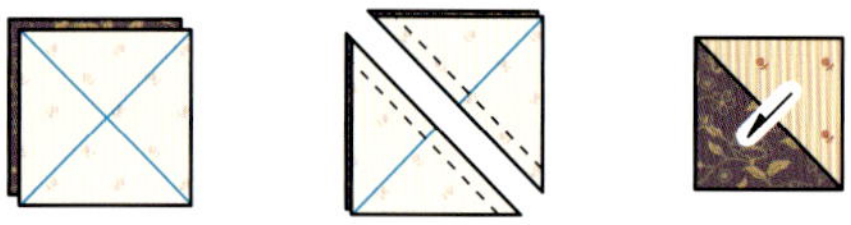

Make 4 units, 2⅞" × 2⅞".

2 Layer two half-square-triangle units right sides together with opposite fabrics facing and the seams abutted. Extend the drawn line on the light print diagonally across the indigo print. Sew a scant ¼" from both sides of the drawn line. Repeat with the remaining half-square-triangle units. Cut the units apart on the drawn line to make four quarter-square-triangle units. Refer to "Clipping Trick" on page 92 to clip the seam intersections. Press the seam allowances toward the indigo print and press the clipped intersections open. Trim each unit to 2½" square.

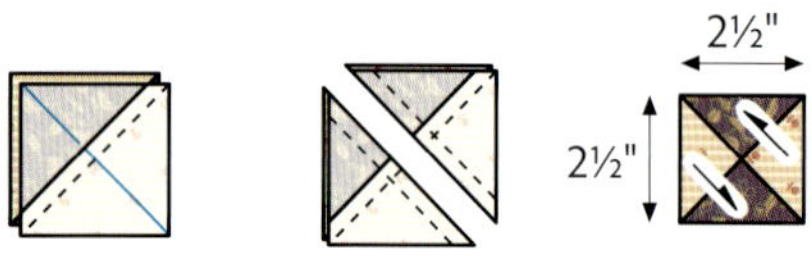

Make 4 units.

3 Arrange the quarter-square-triangle units and the remaining squares in the set into three horizontal rows, making sure the dark triangles in the quarter-square-triangle units adjoin the center square as shown. Sew the pieces together into rows. Join the rows to complete the block. Clip the seam intersections. Press the seam allowances toward the corners and center and press the clipped intersections open. The block should measure 6½" square, including seam allowances.

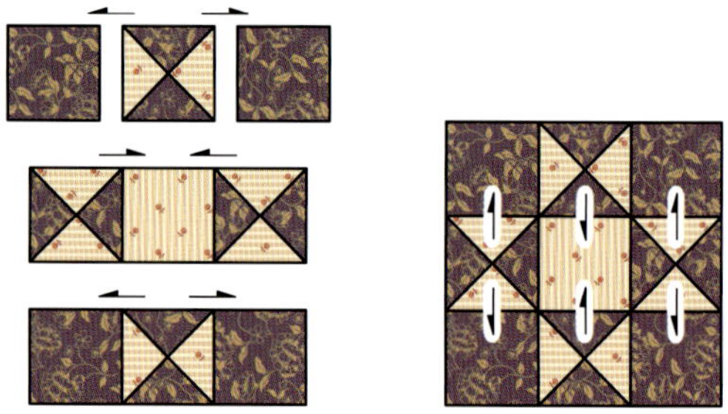

Make 1 block, 6½" × 6½".

4 Repeat steps 1–3 to make a total of 30 blocks.

Making the Inner-Border Strips

1 Draw a diagonal line from corner to corner on the wrong side of each mustard 3" square.

2 Align two marked mustard squares on opposite corners of an indigo 5½" square, right sides together and raw edges aligned; the squares will overlap in the center. Sew a scant ¼" from each side of the drawn lines. Cut the layered squares apart on the drawn lines to yield two heart-shaped units.

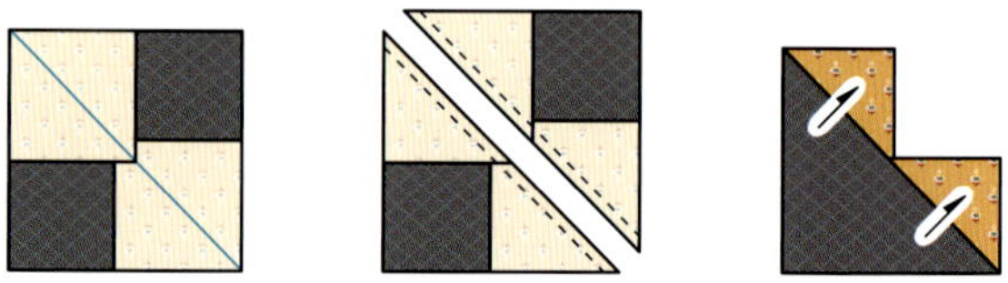

3 Place a marked mustard square on the corner of the indigo triangle of one step 2 unit, noting the direction of the diagonal line. Sew a scant ¼" from each side of the line. Cut on the drawn line. Repeat with the remaining unit from step 2 to make four flying-geese units measuring 2⅝" × 4¾", including seam allowances.

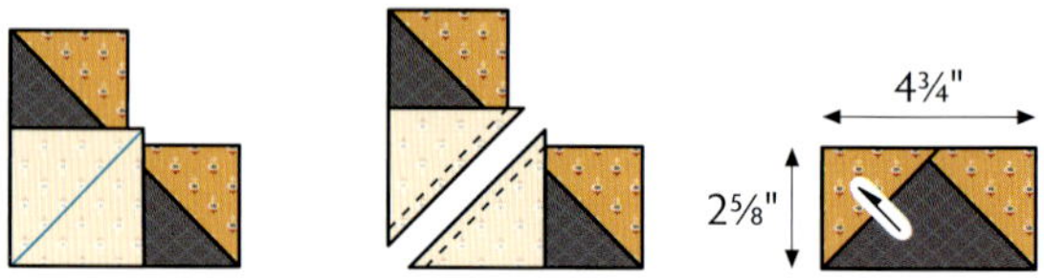

Make 4 units.

By **Jo Morton**; *machine quilted by* **Maggi Honeyman**

4 Repeat steps 2 and 3 to make a total of 44 flying-geese units.

5 Draw a diagonal line from corner to corner on the wrong side of the two mustard 3¼" squares. Layer each marked square on top of an indigo 3¼" square, right sides together. Sew a scant ¼" from each side of the drawn lines. Cut the units apart on the drawn line to make four half-square-triangle units. Trim each unit to measure 2⅝" square.

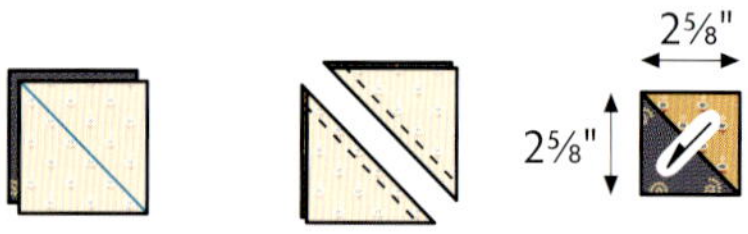

Make 4 units.

6 Sew 12 flying-geese units together as shown to make a side border strip measuring 2⅝" × 51½", including seam allowances. Repeat to make a second side border strip.

Make 2 side borders, 2⅝" × 51½".

7 Sew 10 flying-geese units and two half-square-triangle units together as shown to make the top border strip measuring 2⅝" × 47¼", including seam allowances. Repeat to make the bottom border strip.

Make 2 top/bottom borders, 2⅝" × 47¼".

Assembling the Quilt Top

1 Refer to the quilt assembly diagram below to arrange the blocks and mustard 6½" setting squares into 10 diagonal rows. Add the mustard setting triangles to the edges and corners. Sew the blocks and setting pieces together in each row.

2 Pin and sew the rows together, matching seam intersections. Clip the seam intersections. Press the seam allowances toward the setting squares and triangles and press the clipped intersections open. Add the corner triangles last.

Quilt assembly

3 Trim the edges of the quilt ¼" from the block points. The quilt top should measure 43" × 51½", including seam allowances.

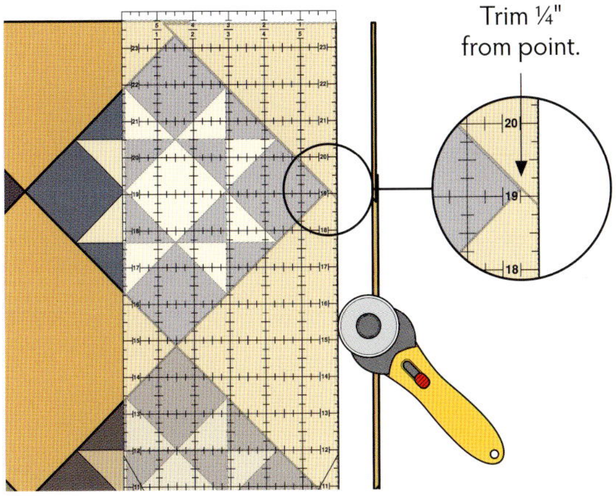

4 Pin and sew the pieced side borders to the quilt. Pin and sew the pieced top and bottom borders to the quilt. The quilt top should measure 47¼" × 55¾", including seam allowances.

5 Pin and sew the 5½" × 55¾" indigo #1 outer-border strips to the sides of the quilt. Join a 5½" indigo #2 square to the ends of each 5½" × 47¼" indigo #1 strip. Pin and sew these outer-border strips to the top and bottom of the quilt, matching seam intersections. Press the seam allowances toward the outer-border strips and press the clipped intersections open. The quilt top should measure 57¼" × 65¾".

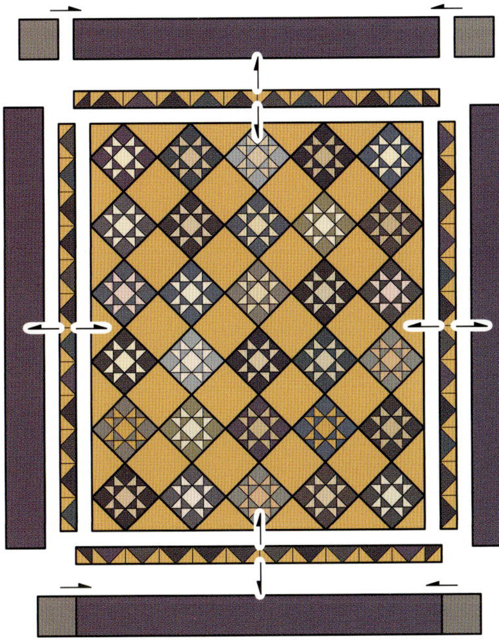

Adding borders

Quilting and Finishing

For more information about any finishing steps, visit ShopMartingale.com/HowtoQuilt.

1 Layer the quilt top, batting, and backing. Baste the layers together.

2 Hand or machine quilt as desired. The quilt shown is machine quilted in the ditch along the block edges. Each block segment is quilted with a curved continuous line. The setting blocks are beautifully quilted with a square feathered wreath, and the setting triangles are filled with a petal design. The inner border is also quilted with a curved continuous line, and both sides of the inner border are quilted in the ditch. A curvy feather design fills the outer border.

3 Use the 1⅛"-wide indigo #3 strips to make single-fold binding; attach the binding to the quilt. For more detailed information about my technique for making the binding and attaching it, see "Single-Fold Binding" on page 94.

Down to the Wire

Making a scrap quilt is like walking down memory lane. As I cut and sew, I remember which fabric collection this piece came from, which quilts that print was used in, and even what publications the previous quilts may have appeared in. I've designed a lot of fabrics, so that's a lot to remember! If your scrap bin is overflowing, you can easily make this quilt larger simply by making more blocks.

Finished Quilt: 41¼" × 51½" **Finished Block:** 7" × 7"

Materials

Yardage is based on 42"-wide fabric.

- 2 yards *total* of assorted dark prints for blocks
- 1 yard *total* of assorted light prints for blocks
- ½ yard of light print for setting squares
- ¾ yard of gray print for setting triangles and single-fold binding
- 1⅓ yards of black print for border
- ¼ yard of brown print for border cornerstones
- 2¾ yards of fabric for backing
- 48" × 58" piece of batting

Cutting

All measurements include ¼" seam allowances.

Cutting for 1 Block

You'll need a total of 12 blocks, but it's easier to cut them one at a time.

From *each* of 2 light prints, cut:
5 squares, 2¼" × 2¼" (10 total)

From *each* of 2 dark prints, cut:
1 square, 4¾" × 4¾"; cut into quarters diagonally to yield 4 side triangles (8 total; 2 from each print are extra)
1 square, 3" × 3"; cut into quarters diagonally to yield 4 end triangles (8 total)
5 squares, 2¼" × 2¼" (10 total)

Cutting for Setting, Border, and Binding

From the light print, cut:
6 squares, 7½" × 7½"

From the gray print, cut:
5 strips, 1⅛" × 42"
3 squares, 11¼" × 11¼"; cut into quarters diagonally to yield 12 setting triangles (2 are extra)
2 squares, 6¼" × 6¼"; cut in half diagonally to yield 4 corner setting triangles

From the black print, cut *along the lengthwise grain*:
2 strips, 6" × 40½"
2 strips, 6" × 30¼"

From the brown print, cut:
4 squares, 6" × 6"

Making the Blocks

Use a scant ¼" seam allowance. Press all seam allowances as shown by the arrows in the illustrations.

1 Select one set of block pieces. Draw a diagonal line from corner to corner on the wrong side of each light 2¼" square. Place a marked square from one light print on a 2¼" square from one dark print. Using the same two light and dark prints, repeat to layer the remaining marked light squares on the remaining dark 2¼" squares. Then layer the other two light and dark prints. Sew a scant ¼" from both sides of the marked lines. Cut the layered squares apart on the drawn lines to make 20 half-square-triangle units (10 units from each pair of light and dark fabrics). Trim the units to measure 1¾" square.

Make 20 units.

2 Lay out five matching half-square-triangle units and two matching end triangles in two rows as shown. Sew the pieces together to make a long row and a short row. Repeat to make a total of two long rows and two short rows.

Make 2 of each row.

3 Pin and sew a short row to the left edge of a matching side triangle. Pin and sew a long row to the top of the side triangle, matching the seam intersection. Refer to "Clipping Trick" on page 92 to clip the seam intersection. Press the seam allowances toward the side triangle and press the clipped intersection open. Repeat to make a total of two matching pieced triangles.

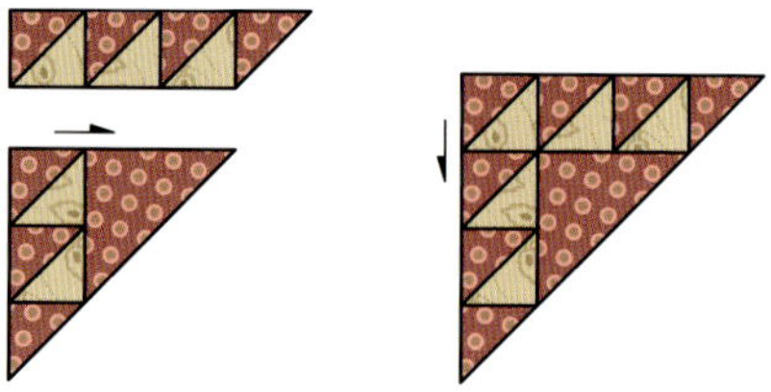

Make 2 units.

4 Repeat steps 2 and 3 with the half-square-triangle units, end triangles, and side triangles from the remaining dark print to make two matching pieced triangles.

5 Lay out the pieced triangles as shown. Pin and sew the triangles together in pairs, matching seam intersections. Clip the seam intersections. Press the seam allowances toward the darker fabric and press the clipped intersections open. Pin and sew the pairs, matching seam intersections; clip and press as before. The block should measure 7½" square, including seam allowances.

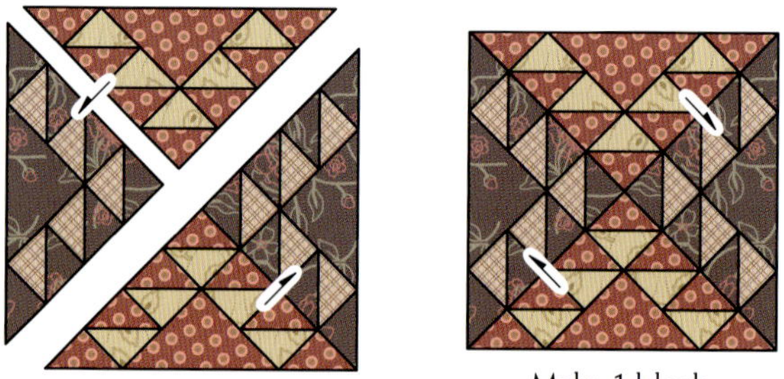

Make 1 block, 7½" × 7½".

6 Repeat steps 1–5 to make a total of 12 blocks.

By ***Jo Morton***

Assembling the Quilt Top

1 Refer to the quilt assembly diagram below to arrange the blocks and light 7½" squares into six diagonal rows. Rearrange the blocks until you're satisfied with the color placement. Add the gray setting triangles to the edges and corners. Sew the blocks and setting pieces together in each row.

2 Pin and sew the rows together, matching seam intersections. Clip the seam intersections. Press the seam allowances toward the setting squares and triangles and press the clipped intersections open. Add the corner triangles last.

3 Trim the edges of the quilt ¼" from the block points. The quilt top should measure 30¼" × 40½", including seam allowances.

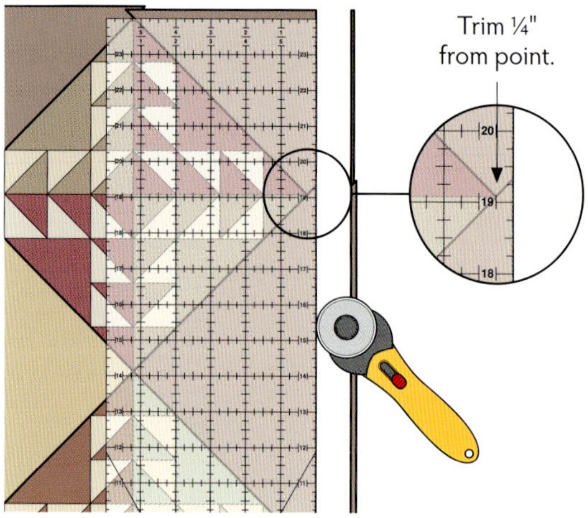

Quilt assembly

4 Pin and sew the black 6" × 40½" border strips to the sides of the quilt. Sew the brown 6" squares to the ends of each black 6" × 30¼" border strip. Pin; sew these border strips to the top and bottom of the quilt. Clip the seam intersections. Press the seam allowances toward the border, press the cornerstones toward the side borders, and press the clipped intersections open. The quilt top should measure 41¼" × 51½".

Adding the border

Quilting and Finishing

For more information about any finishing steps, visit ShopMartingale.com/HowtoQuilt.

1 Layer the quilt top, batting, and backing. Baste the layers together.

2 Hand or machine quilt as desired. The quilt shown is quilted in the ditch around each block. Concentric squares are stitched inside each block, with lines established by the half-square triangles. The setting squares are quilted with a feathered X, and the setting triangles are echo quilted with lines spaced about ⅞" apart. The border corner squares feature a crosshatch design, and the remainder of the border is quilted with a feather design.

3 Use the gray 1⅛"-wide strips to make single-fold binding; attach the binding to the quilt. For more detailed information about my technique for making the binding and attaching it, see "Single-Fold Binding" on page 94.

16 Patch Strippy

We all need a stress-free project to work on now and then, don't we? So if you're like me and believe that even the smallest scraps can find a home somewhere, you'll want to make this quilt. It's great for tiny leftovers, and there's nothing complicated about it. With vertical rows of blocks separated by sashing strips, this is also the perfect place to use a favorite striped fabric.

Finished Quilt: 42¾" × 52½" **Finished Block:** 4" × 4"

Materials

Yardage is based on 42"-wide fabric.

- ⅞ yard *total* of assorted light prints for blocks
- ⅞ yard *total* of assorted dark prints for blocks
- ½ yard of brick red print for setting rectangles
- 1⅔ yards of tan stripe for sashing and borders
- 1⅔ yards of dark brown stripe for sashing and binding
- 2¾ yards of fabric for backing
- 49" × 59" piece of batting

Cutting

All measurements include ¼" seam allowances.

From the assorted light prints, cut a *total* of:
320 squares, 1½" × 1½"

From the assorted dark prints, cut a *total* of:
320 squares, 1½" × 1½"

From the brick red print, cut:
40 rectangles, 2½" × 4½"

From the tan stripe, fussy cut *along the lengthwise grain*:
2 strips, 6" × 52½"
2 strips, 2⅜" × 48½"
2 strips, 2½" × 31¾"

From the dark brown stripe, cut:
5 strips, 1⅛" × 42"

From the remaining dark brown stripe, fussy cut *along the lengthwise grain*:
2 strips, 4¼" × 48½"

Making the Blocks

Use a scant ¼" seam allowance. Press all seam allowances as shown by the arrows in the illustrations.

Randomly select eight light and eight dark 1½" squares. Lay out the squares in four rows of four squares each, alternating the light and dark squares as shown. Sew the squares together in each row. Pin and sew the rows together, matching seam intersections. Refer to "Clipping Trick" on page 92 to clip the seam intersections. Press the seam allowances toward the dark squares and press the clipped intersections open. The block should measure 4½" square, including seam allowances. Repeat to make a total of 40 blocks.

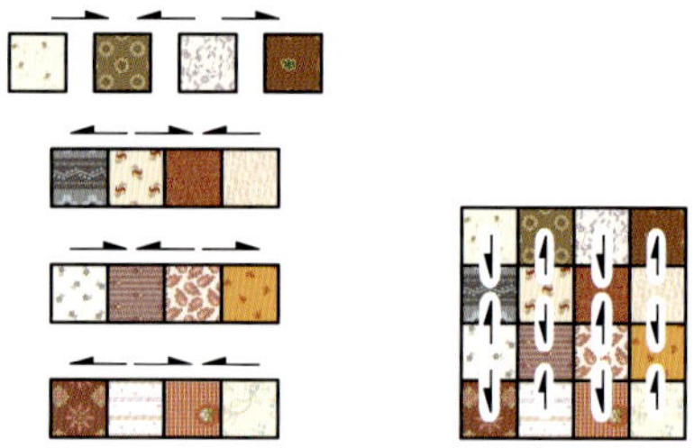

Make 40 blocks,
4½" × 4½".

Assembling the Quilt Top

1 Sew eight blocks and eight brick red 2½" × 4½" rectangles into a row as shown. The row should measure 4½" × 48½", including seam allowances. Repeat to make a total of five block rows.

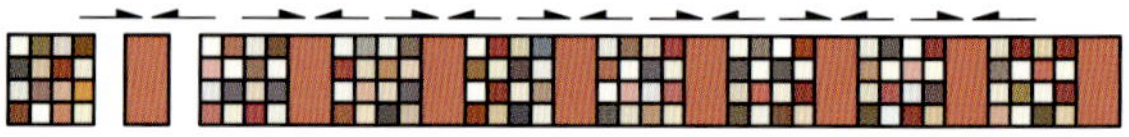

Make 5 rows,
4½" × 48½".

2 Refer to the quilt assembly diagram on page 48 to lay out the block rows, the tan stripe 2⅜" × 48½" strips, and the dark brown stripe 4¼" × 48½" strips. Pin and sew the rows and strips together. The quilt top should measure 31¾" × 48½", including seam allowances.

*By **Jo Morton;** machine quilted by **Maggi Honeyman***

3 Pin and sew the tan stripe 2½" × 31¾" strips to the top and bottom of the quilt. Pin and sew the tan stripe 6" × 52½" strips to the sides of the quilt. The quilt top should measure 42¾" × 52½".

Quilting and Finishing

For more information about any finishing steps, visit ShopMartingale.com/HowtoQuilt.

1 Layer the quilt top, batting, and backing. Baste the layers together.

2 Hand or machine quilt as desired. The quilt shown is machine quilted with an X through each quadrant of the 16 Patch blocks and a crosshatch design on each rectangle of the block strips. The striped strips are quilted with vertical lines that outline the stripes in the fabric. The border features a crosshatch design, with lines spaced about ¾" apart.

3 Use the dark brown stripe 1⅛"-wide strips to make single-fold binding; attach the binding to the quilt. For more detailed information about my technique for making the binding and attaching it, see "Single-Fold Binding" on page 94.

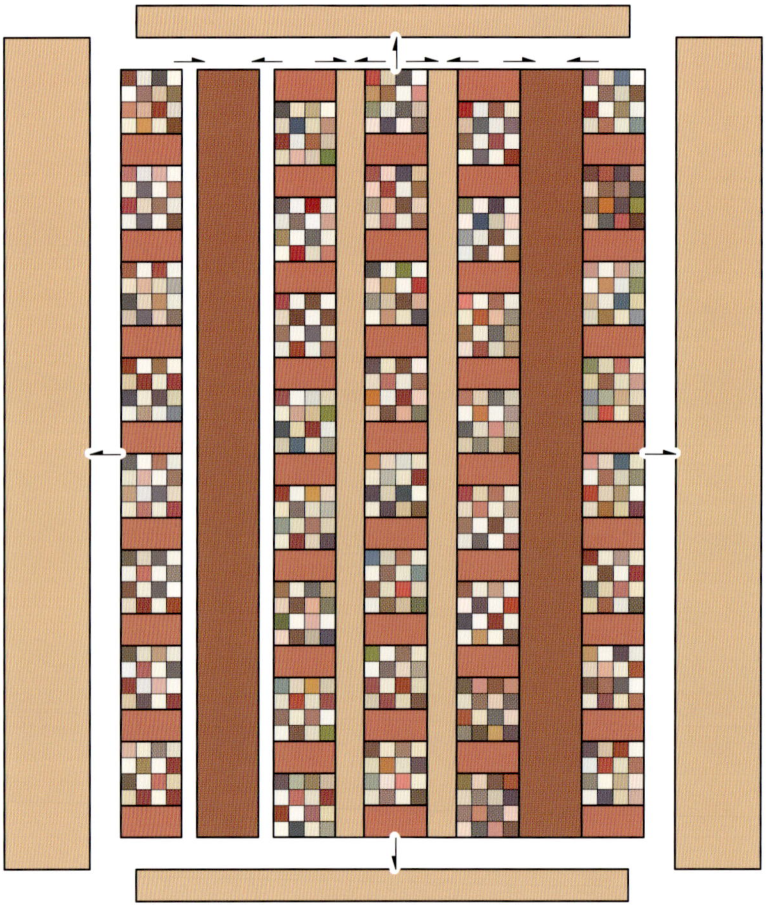

Quilt assembly

Peppermint Twist

By now you know I'm a big fan of brown, but have I mentioned that I *love* pink and brown together? This originally started out as just a Churn Dash quilt with each block made from a pink, a brown, and a cream fabric. Then I designed the center appliquéd block, which led to the pieced border around it, which led to an outer border that echoed it. You know how it goes. Sometimes more is better!

Finished Quilt: 36½" × 36½" **Finished Center Block:** 11¼" × 11¼" **Finished Churn Dash Block:** 4" × 4"

Materials

Yardage is based on 42"-wide fabric. Fat quarters are 18" × 21".

- ⅝ yard *total* of assorted light prints for blocks
- ⅓ yard *total* of assorted brown prints for blocks and appliqués
- ¼ yard *total* of assorted pink prints for blocks and appliqués
- 1 fat quarter of cream print for appliquéd block
- ½ yard of brown floral for appliquéd block, border, and single-fold binding
- 1 yard of pink dot for appliqués, setting pieces, and outer border
- 1¼ yards of fabric for backing
- 43" × 43" square of batting
- Supplies for your favorite appliqué method

Cutting

All measurements include ¼" seam allowances. For each Churn Dash block, select one light, one brown, and one pink print.

Cutting for 1 Block

You'll need a total of 32 blocks, but it's easier to cut them one at a time.

From the light print, cut:
2 squares, 2⅜" × 2⅜"
1 strip, 1¼" × 7"
1 square, 1½" × 1½"

From the brown print, cut:
2 squares, 2⅜" × 2⅜"

From the pink print, cut:
1 strip, 1¼" × 7"

Continued on page 51

Continued from page 49

Cutting for Appliquéd Block, Setting, Border, and Binding

From the cream print, cut:

1 square, 11" × 11"
32 squares, 1½" × 1½"

From the brown floral, cut:

4 strips, 1⅞" × 42"; crosscut into 68 squares, 1⅞" × 1⅞"
4 strips, 1⅛" × 42"; from *1* strip, cut 4 squares, 1⅛" × 1⅛"
8 squares, 2½" × 2½"
4 squares, 1½" × 1½"

From the pink dot, cut:

7 squares, 7¼" × 7¼"; cut into quarters diagonally to yield 28 setting triangles
16 squares, 4½" × 4½"
4 squares, 4" × 4"; cut in half diagonally to yield 8 setting and corner triangles
17 squares, 3¼" × 3¼"

Making the Appliquéd Block

Use your favorite appliqué method or refer to "Back-Basting Needle-Turn Appliqué" on page 92. When piecing and adding the border, use a scant ¼" seam allowance. Press all seam allowances as shown by the arrows in the illustrations.

1 Prepare the appliqués listed below using patterns A–G on page 56 and referring to the photo on page 52 for fabric colors.

- 1 of A (stem) ***Note:*** If you're not using my back-basting appliqué technique, you'll need to make about 21" of ¼"-wide finished bias strip.
- 27 of B (leaf)
- 1 of C (star)
- 1 of D (large circle)
- 1 of E (small circle)
- 1 of F (flower center)
- 1 of G (flower petal)

2 Place the appliqué shapes on the cream 11" square. Pin or baste the pieces in place.

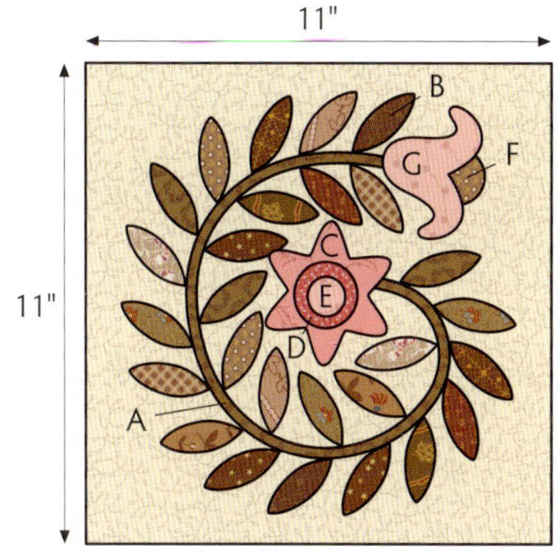

Appliqué placement

3 Appliqué the shapes in place by hand or machine.

4 Trim the appliquéd square to measure 10½" square, keeping the design centered.

5 Draw a diagonal line from corner to corner on the wrong side of each cream 1½" square.

6 Align two marked squares on opposite corners of a brown 2½" square, right sides together and raw edges aligned. The squares will overlap in the center. Sew a scant ¼" from each side of the drawn lines. Cut the layered squares apart on the lines to yield two heart-shaped units.

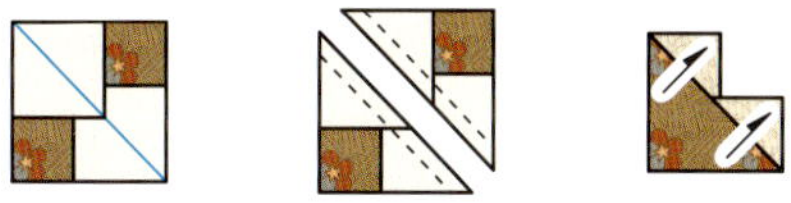

7 Place a marked cream square on the corner of the brown triangle of a step 6 unit, noting the direction of the diagonal line. Sew a scant ¼" from each side of the drawn line. Cut the unit apart on the drawn line. Repeat with the remaining unit from step 6 to make four flying-geese units measuring 1⅛" × 1¾", including seam allowances.

Make 4 units, 1⅛" × 1¾".

Designed by ***Jo Morton****; pieced by* ***Jo Morton, Mary Fornoff, Cindy Hansen,*** *and* ***Phyllis Masters****; machine quilted by* ***Maggi Honeyman***

8 Repeat steps 6 and 7 to make a total of 32 flying-geese units.

9 Sew eight flying-geese units together end to end as shown to make a pieced strip. The strip should measure 1⅛" × 10½", including seam allowances. Repeat to make a total of four pieced strips.

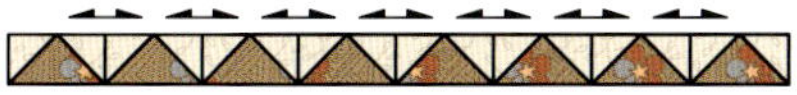

Make 4 strips, 1⅛" × 10½".

10 Pin and sew a flying-geese strip to opposite sides of the appliquéd square, making sure the cream fabric adjoins the square. Sew brown 1⅛" squares to the ends of the two remaining pieced strips. Pin and sew these strips to the top and bottom of the appliquéd square. The appliquéd block should measure 11¾" square, including seam allowances.

Appliquéd block assembly

Making the Churn Dash Blocks

Use a scant ¼" seam allowance. Press all seam allowances as shown by the arrows.

1 Select one set of block pieces. Draw a diagonal line from corner to corner on the wrong side of each light 2⅜" square.

2 Layer a marked square with a brown 2⅜" square, right sides together. Sew a scant ¼" from each side of the drawn line. Cut the layered squares apart on the drawn line to make two half-square-triangle units. Repeat to make a total of four units. Trim the units to measure 2" square.

Make 4 units.

3 Sew the light and pink 1¼" × 7" strips together along the long edges to make a strip set. Crosscut the strip set into four segments, 1½" wide.

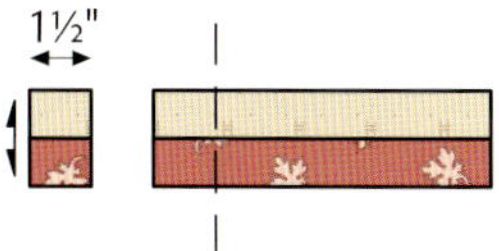

Make 1 strip set, 2" × 7".
Cut 4 segments, 1½" × 2".

4 Arrange the half-square-triangle units, the strip-set segments, and the light 1½" square in three horizontal rows as shown on page 54. Sew the pieces together in each row. Pin and sew the rows together, matching seam intersections. Refer to "Clipping Trick" on page 92 to clip the seam intersections. Press the seam allowances toward the strip-set segments and press the clipped intersections open. The block should measure 4½" square, including seam allowances.

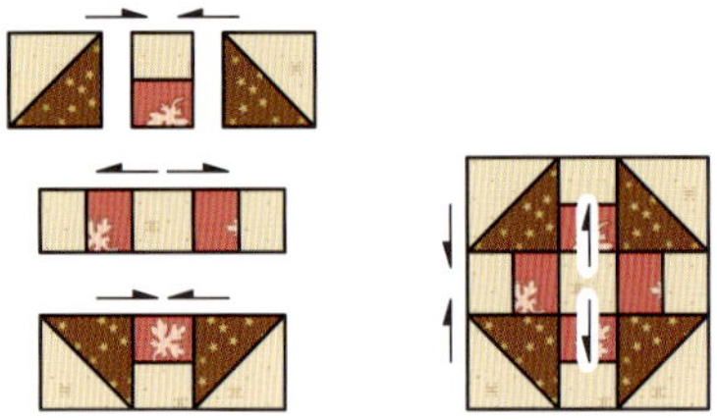

Make 1 block, 4½" × 4½".

5 Repeat steps 1–4 to make a total of 32 blocks.

Assembling the Quilt Top

1 Refer to the quilt assembly diagram below to arrange the blocks and pink dot 4½" setting squares and setting triangles into 11 diagonal rows, leaving room in the center to place the appliquéd block. Add the remaining setting triangles to the edges and corners. Separate the pieces into eight sections as shown. Sew the pieces together in each section, matching seam intersections. Clip the seam intersections. Press the seam allowances toward the setting pieces and press the clipped intersections open.

2 Pin and sew the sections above and below the appliquéd block to the top and bottom of the block. Pin and sew the sections on each side of the appliquéd block to the sides of the block.

3 Pin and then sew the lower-left and upper-right sections to opposite sides of the quilt, matching seam intersections. Clip the seam intersections. Press the seam allowances toward the setting pieces. Pin and sew the upper-left and lower-right sections to the remaining sides of the quilt, matching seam intersections. Clip and press as before. In order for the border strips to fit, the quilt top should measure 34½" square, including seam allowances. You may need to take in or let out a few seams to achieve the correct dimensions.

Quilt assembly

Adding the Border

1 Using the brown 1⅞" squares and pink dot 3¼" squares, refer to steps 5–7 of "Making the Appliquéd Block" to make a total of 68 flying-geese units measuring 1½" × 2½", including seam allowances.

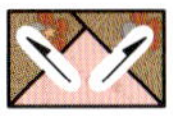

Make 68 units, 1½" × 2½".

2 Sew 17 flying-geese units together end to end to make a pieced strip. The strip should measure 1½" × 34½", including seam allowances. Repeat to make a total of four pieced strips.

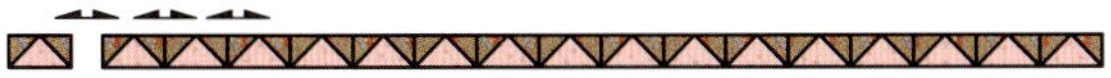

Make 4 strips, 1½" × 34½".

3 Pin and sew two flying-geese strips to opposite sides of the quilt, making sure the pink fabric adjoins the top. Sew a brown 1½" square to the ends of the two remaining pieced strips. Pin and sew these strips to the top and bottom of the quilt. The quilt top should measure 36½" square.

Adding the border

Quilting and Finishing

For more information about any finishing steps, visit ShopMartingale.com/HowtoQuilt.

1 Layer the quilt top, batting, and backing. Baste the layers together.

2 Hand or machine quilt as desired. The quilt shown is stipple quilted in the background of the appliquéd block, and quilted details are added to the appliqués. The blocks, the border around the appliquéd block, and the outer border are stitched in the ditch. The setting squares and side setting triangles have feathered wreaths, and each corner triangle has a quarter feathered wreath.

3 Use the brown 1⅛"-wide strips to make single-fold binding; attach the binding to the quilt. For more detailed information about my technique for making the binding and attaching it, see "Single-Fold Binding" on page 94.

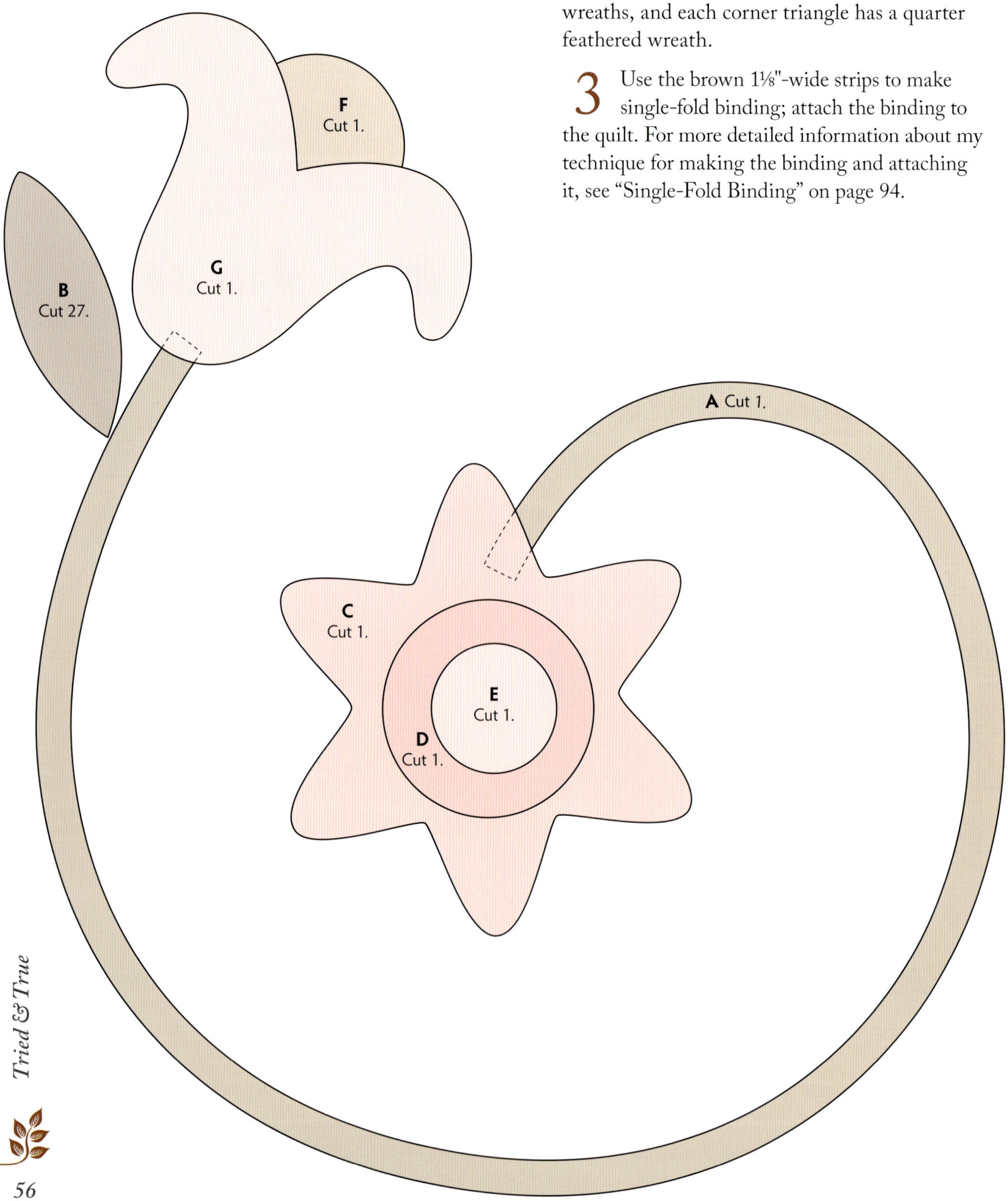

Triangles in a Row

Scrappy quilts were quite common before the turn of the twentieth century. Women used what they had on hand, including recycled garments, to make quilts. Quilters didn't have the luxury of going to a store with thousands of bolts, but they did often trade fabrics with friends for more variety. If your scrap bin is overflowing or if you just want to put a dent in your fabric collection, this quilt is perfect. The eight-at-a-time method makes quick work of the triangle units.

Finished Quilt: 60" x 74½"

Materials

Yardage is based on 42"-wide fabric.

- 2⅓ yards *total* of assorted light prints for half-square-triangle units and large triangles
- 5 yards *total* of assorted medium and dark prints for half-square-triangle units and large and small triangles (collectively referred to as *dark*)
- ⅓ yard of rust paisley print for single-fold binding
- 3¾ yards of fabric for backing
- 66" × 81" piece of batting

Cutting

All measurements include ¼" seam allowances.

From the assorted light prints, cut a *total* of:
84 squares, 5" × 5"

From the assorted dark prints, cut a *total* of:
84 squares, 5" × 5"
60 squares, 3⅜" × 3⅜"; cut into quarters diagonally to yield 240 small triangles

From the assorted light and dark prints, cut a *total* of:
60 squares, 7⅝" × 7⅝"; cut into quarters diagonally to yield 240 large triangles

From the rust paisley print, cut:
7 strips, 1⅛" × 42"

Making the Half-Square-Triangle Units

Use a scant ¼" seam allowance. Press all seam allowances as shown by the arrows in the illustrations.

1 Draw a diagonal line from corner to corner in both directions on the wrong side of each light 5" square, creating an X.

2 Layer a marked light square right sides together with a dark 5" square. Sew a scant ¼" from both sides of each line. Cut the layered squares into quarters horizontally and vertically,

and then cut on the drawn lines to make eight half-square-triangle units. Carefully press each unit and trim to 2" square. Repeat to make a total of 672 units.

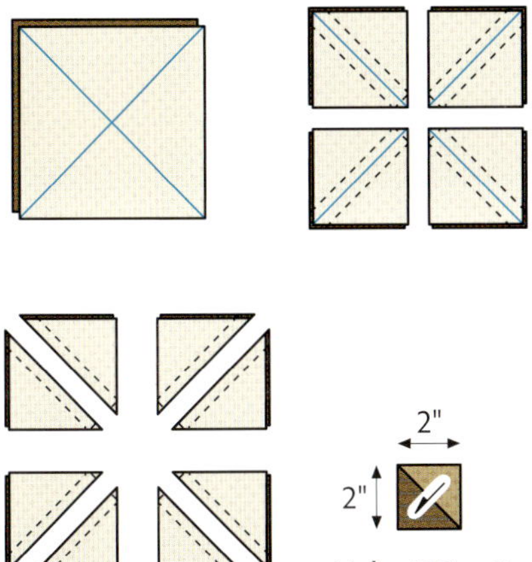

Make 672 units.

Assembling the Quilt Top

1 Sew three half-square-triangle units together side by side, positioning the slant of the triangles as shown. Join a small triangle to the left end of the row to make an A unit. Repeat to make a total of 112 units.

Make 112 A units.

2 Sew three half-square-triangle units together side by side, noting the different direction of the slant. Join a small triangle to the left end of the row to make a B unit. Repeat to make a total of 112 units.

Make 112 B units.

3 Pin and sew an A unit to the left edge of a large triangle. Pin and sew a B unit to the right edge of the triangle, matching seam intersections. Refer to "Clipping Trick" on page 92 to clip the seam intersection. Press the seam allowances toward the large and small

triangles and press the clipped intersection open. Repeat to make a total of 112 pieced triangles.

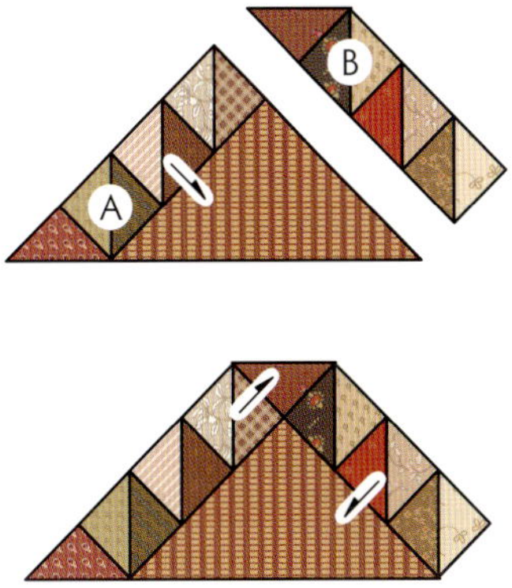

Make 112 units.

4 Refer to the quilt assembly diagram on page 61 to lay out the pieced triangles and remaining large and small triangles into 16 rows of seven pieced triangles, eight large triangles, and one small triangle each. Rearrange the pieces until you're satisfied with the color placement.

5 Working on one row at a time, sew each pieced triangle to the adjacent large triangle to the right to make a unit. Sew the units together, matching seam intersections. Clip the seam intersections. Press the seam allowances toward the large and small triangles and press the clipped intersections open. Add the large triangle on the left end of the row and the small triangle on the right end of the row last.

Make 16 rows.

By ***Jo Morton;*** *machine quilted by* ***Maggi Honeyman***

6 Pin the rows together, keeping the points of the large triangles aligned vertically from row to row. Then sew the rows together and clip the seam intersections. Press the seam allowances toward the large triangles and press the clipped intersections open.

7 Trim the edges of the quilt ¼" from the point of the lowermost half-square-triangle unit of each pieced triangle. The quilt top should measure 60" × 74½".

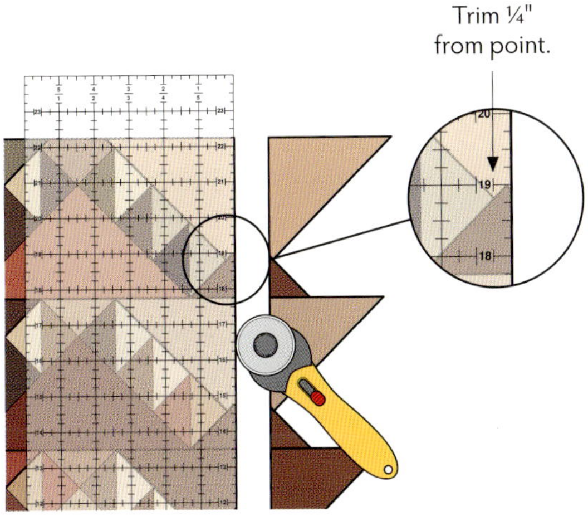

Quilting and Finishing

For more information about any finishing steps, visit ShopMartingale.com/HowtoQuilt.

1 Layer the quilt top, batting, and backing. Baste the layers together.

2 Hand or machine quilt as desired. The quilt shown is machine quilted with an allover meandering pattern.

3 Use the rust paisley 1⅛"-wide strips to make single-fold binding; attach the binding to the quilt. For more detailed information about my technique for making the binding and attaching it, see "Single-Fold Binding" on page 94.

Quilt assembly

Love Apple Medallion

Sometimes you fall in love with a block and find yourself using it over and over again. Such is the case with the T block in this quilt. I've used it multiple times in a variety of sizes over the years. And now here it is again! T blocks make a perfect backdrop for the appliquéd Love Apple (pomegranate) block, and doesn't the blue polka dot make everything sing? I just love this quilt and hope you do too.

Finished Quilt: 61½" × 61½" **Finished Love Apple Block:** 13" × 13" **Finished T Blocks:** 3¾" × 3¾"

Materials

Yardage is based on 42"-wide fabric. Fat quarters are 18" × 21".

- 1¾ yards *total* of assorted dark prints for blocks and appliqués
- 1⅔ yards *total* of assorted light prints for blocks
- 1 fat quarter of tan paisley print for Love Apple block background
- ¼ yard *total* of assorted shirting prints for Love Apple block inner border
- ⅜ yard *total* of assorted brown prints for Love Apple block inner border and appliqués
- ⅛ yard of brown-and-pink stripe for Love Apple block outer border
- ½ yard of dark blue polka dot for setting triangles and inner border
- 1 yard of tan dotted print for setting squares and triangles
- ½ yard of brown paisley print for setting triangles
- ½ yard of medium blue print for inner border
- ⅞ yard of brown-and-pink paisley stripe for outer border
- ⅓ yard of rust print for binding
- 3⅞ yards of fabric for backing
- 68" × 68" square of batting

Cutting

All measurements include ¼" seam allowances. For each Baby T block, select one light print and one dark print.

Cutting for 1 Baby T Block

You'll need a total of 72 blocks, but it's easier to cut them one at a time.

From the dark print, cut:

4 squares, 1⅝" × 1⅝"; cut in half diagonally to make 8 triangles

4 rectangles, 1¼" × 2"

From the light print, cut:

2 squares, 2⅜" × 2⅜"; cut in half diagonally to make 4 triangles

5 squares, 1¼" × 1¼"

Continued on page 64

Continued from page 63

Cutting for Love Apple Block, Setting Pieces, Borders, and Binding

From the tan paisley print, cut:
1 square, 14" × 14"

From the assorted shirting prints, cut a *total* of:
26 squares, 2" × 2"

From the assorted brown prints, cut a *total* of:
26 squares, 2" × 2"

From the brown-and-pink stripe, cut:
2 strips, 1" × 16½"
2 strips, 1" × 15½"

From the dark blue polka dot, cut:
11 squares, 6⅝" × 6⅝"; cut into quarters diagonally to yield 44 triangles
4 squares, 3⅛" × 3⅛"

From the tan dotted print, cut:
1 square, 6⅝" × 6⅝"; cut into quarters diagonally to yield 4 large triangles
48 squares, 4¼" × 4¼"
2 squares, 3½" × 3½"; cut in half diagonally to yield 4 small triangles

From the brown paisley print, cut:
8 squares, 6⅝" × 6⅝"; cut into quarters diagonally to yield 32 large triangles
2 squares, 3½" × 3½"; cut in half diagonally to yield 4 small triangles

From the medium blue print, cut:
8 squares, 6⅝" × 6⅝"; cut into quarters diagonally to yield 32 large triangles
4 squares, 3½" × 3½"; cut in half diagonally to yield 8 small triangles

From the brown-and-pink paisley stripe, cut:
6 strips, 4½" × 42"

From the rust print, cut:
7 strips, 1⅛" × 42"

Making the Quilt Center

Use your favorite appliqué method or, if desired, refer to my tips for adding the appliqués by hand in "Back-Basting Needle-Turn Appliqué" on page 92. When piecing and adding the border, use a scant ¼" seam allowance. Press all seam allowances as shown by the arrows in the illustrations.

1 Prepare the appliqués listed below using patterns A–F on page 69 and referring to the photo on page 65 for fabric colors.

- 2 of A (stem) Note: If you're not using my back-basting appliqué technique, you'll need to make approximately 19" of a ¼"-wide finished bias strip.
- 4 of B (apple bottom)
- 4 of C (apple center)
- 4 of D (apple top)
- 8 of E (rounded leaf)
- 4 of F (pointed leaf)

2 Place the appliqué shapes on the tan 14" square. Pin or baste the pieces in place.

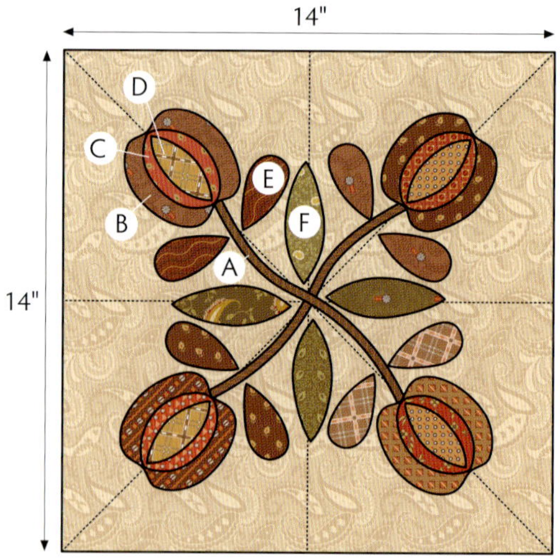

Appliqué placement

3 Appliqué the shapes in place by hand or machine.

By **Jo Morton;** *quilted by* **Maggi Honeyman**

4 Trim the appliquéd block to 13½" square, keeping the design centered.

5 Draw a diagonal line from corner to corner on the wrong side of each shirting 2" square. Layer a marked square with a brown 2" square, right sides together. Sew a scant ¼" from both sides of the drawn line. Cut layered squares apart on the line to make two half-square-triangle units. Repeat to make a total of 52 units. Press and trim each unit to measure 1½" square.

Make 52 units.

6 Arrange 12 half-square-triangle units as shown for each of the side border strips. Sew the units together using a *scant* ¼" seam allowance. In order for the strips to fit the quilt top, they'll need to measure 1½" × 13½", including seam allowances. You may need to let out a few seams to achieve the correct length. Make a total of two side border strips. Sew 14 half-square-triangle units together as shown to make the top border strip measuring 1½" × 15½", including seam allowances. Again, you may need to let out a few seams to achieve the correct length. Repeat to make a bottom border strip.

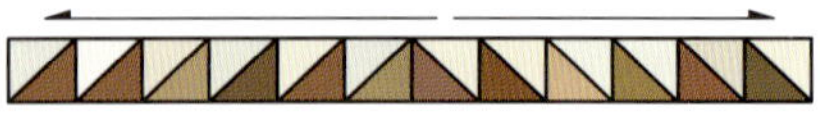
Make 2 side borders,
1½" × 13½".

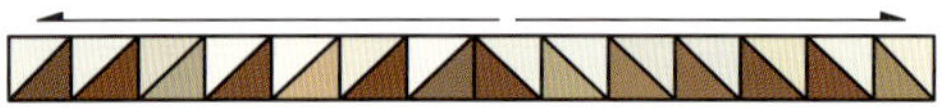
Make 2 side borders,
1½" × 15½".

7 Refer to the quilt center assembly diagram above right to pin and sew the pieced side-border strips to opposite sides of the appliquéd square, making sure the brown prints adjoin the square. Pin and sew the top and bottom pieced border strips to the remaining sides of the square, matching seam intersections. Refer to "Clipping Trick" on page 92 to clip the seam intersections. Press the seam allowances toward the center square and press the clipped intersections open. The center block should measure 15½" square, including seam allowances.

8 Pin and sew the brown-and-pink stripe 1" × 15½" strips to opposite sides of the quilt center. Pin and sew the brown-and-pink stripe 1" × 16½" strips to the remaining sides of the quilt center. The quilt center should measure 16½" square, including seam allowances.

Quilt center assembly

Making the Baby T Blocks

1 Select one set of block pieces. Sew the dark triangles to adjacent sides of a light 1¼" square. Pin and sew a light triangle to the long edge of the unit. Trim the unit to measure 2" square, including seam allowances. Repeat to make a total of four units.

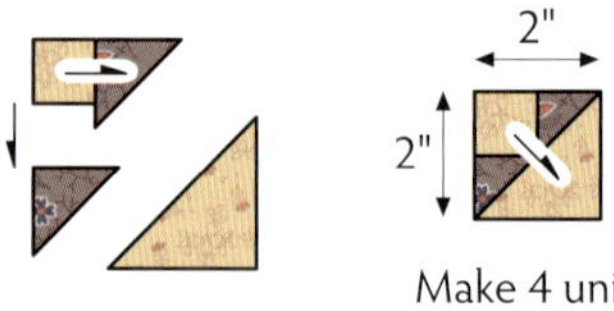

Make 4 units.

2 Arrange the units from step 1 with the remaining pieces in the block set into three horizontal rows. Sew the pieces in each row together. Pin and sew the rows together, matching seam intersections. Clip the seam intersections. Press the seam allowances toward the rectangles and press the clipped intersections open. The block should measure 4¼" square, including seam allowances.

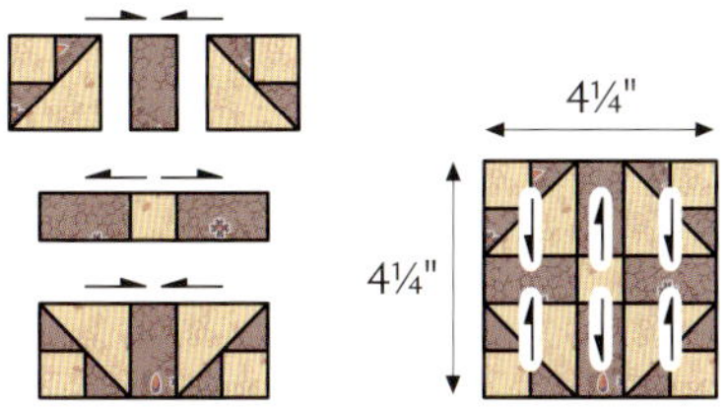

Make 1 block.

3 Repeat steps 1 and 2 to make a total of 72 blocks.

Assembling the Quilt Top

1 Refer to the quilt assembly diagram below to arrange the Baby T blocks, the dark blue polka-dot setting triangles, and tan dotted print 4¼" setting squares and setting triangles into 17 diagonal rows, leaving room in the center to place the appliquéd block. Add the brown paisley setting triangles to the edges and corners. Separate the pieces into eight sections as shown. Sew the pieces together in each section, matching seam intersections. Clip the seam intersections. Press the seam allowances toward the setting pieces and press the clipped intersections open.

2 Pin and sew the sections above and below the appliquéd block to the top and bottom of the block. Pin and sew the sections on each side of the appliquéd block to the sides of the block.

3 Pin and sew the lower-left and upper-right sections to opposite sides of the quilt, matching seam intersections. Clip the seam

Quilt assembly

intersections. Press the seam allowances toward the setting pieces. Pin and sew the upper-left and lower-right sections to the remaining sides of the quilt, matching seam intersections. Clip and press as before.

4 Trim the edges of the quilt ¼" from the block points. The quilt top should measure 48¼" square, including seam allowances.

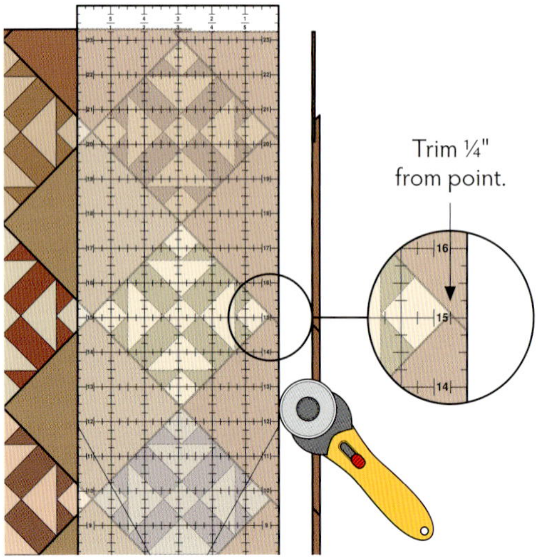

Adding the Borders

1 Sew nine dark blue polka-dot triangles and eight medium blue large triangles together in a row. Add a blue dotted small triangle to each end of the row to make an inner-border strip. Repeat to make a total of four inner-border strips measuring 3⅛" × 48¼", including seam allowances.

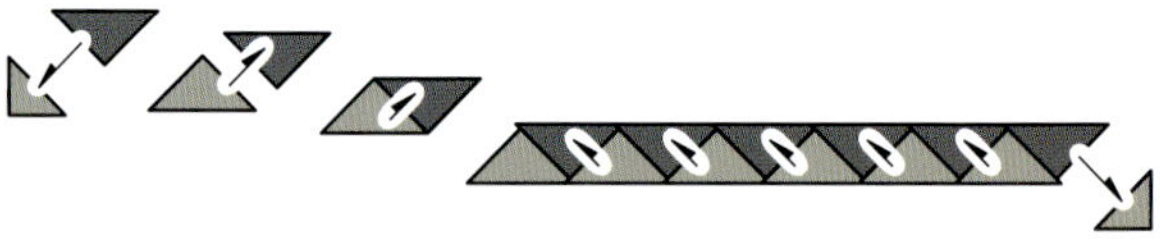

Make 4 inner-border strips, 3⅛" × 48¼".

2 Pin and sew two border strips to opposite sides of the quilt, with the medium blue triangles adjacent to the quilt center. Add dark blue polka-dot 3⅛" squares to the ends of the two remaining strips. Pin and sew these strips to the top and bottom of the quilt, matching seam intersections. Clip the seam intersections. Press the seam allowances toward the border strips and press the clipped intersections open. The quilt top should measure 53½" square, including seam allowances.

3 Piece the paisley stripe 4½" × 42" strips together, matching the print as best as you can, to make one long strip. From the pieced strip, cut two 53½"-long strips and two 61½"-long strips. Pin and sew the two shorter border strips to opposite sides of the quilt. Pin and sew the two longer border strips to the top and bottom of the quilt. The quilt top should measure 61½" square.

Adding borders

Quilting and Finishing

For more information about any finishing steps, visit ShopMartingale.com/HowtoQuilt.

1 Layer the quilt top, batting, and backing. Baste the layers together.

2 Hand or machine quilt as desired. In the quilt shown, the borders of the appliquéd block and the Baby T blocks are machine stitched in the ditch. Each setting square has a feathered wreath. The brown paisley setting triangles and blue dot inner border triangles are treated as one and quilted with a feathered circle, and the dark blue setting triangles and inner border triangles are quilted with half of the same feathered circle. A crosshatch design is quilted in the outer border.

3 Use the rust 1⅛"-wide strips to make single-fold binding; attach the binding to the quilt. For more detailed information about my technique for making the binding and attaching it, see "Single-Fold Binding" on page 94.

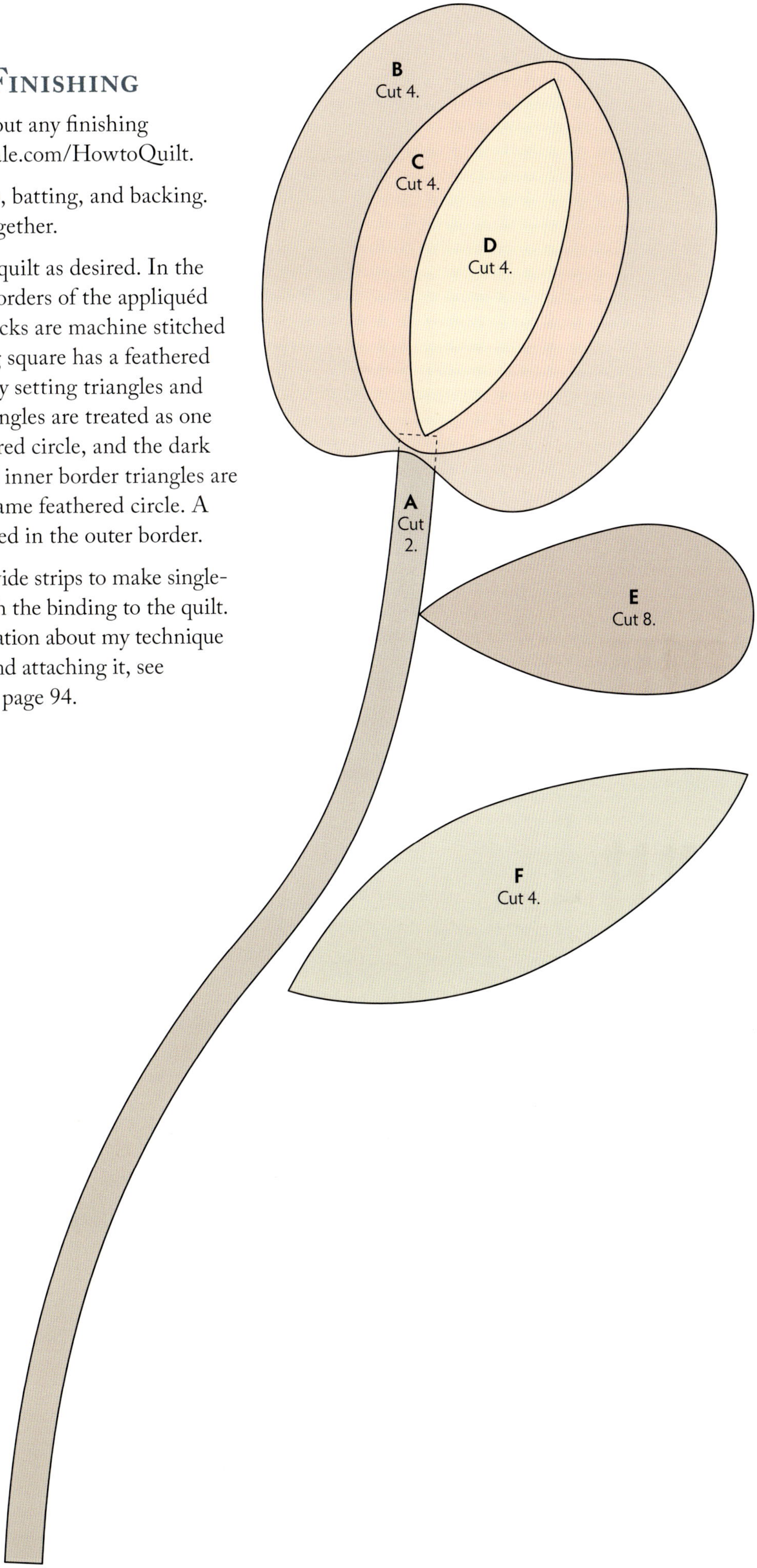

Missouri Crossing

Red-and-green quilts were popular during the nineteenth century, and while they're perfect for the holidays, you don't have to put them in storage the rest of the year. I like to hang this one over the door of a large cupboard in which I display folded quilts. The Ocean Waves block creates movement throughout the quilt, and while the block looks complicated, it's really not. There's no need to tell your friends that, though!

Finished Quilt: 66½" × 66½" **Finished Block:** 6" × 6"

Materials

Yardage is based on 42"-wide fabric.

- 2⅓ yards of cream print for blocks and second border
- 1⅝ yards of small-scale red floral for blocks and first border
- 1 yard *total* of assorted red prints for blocks
- 2 yards of green sprig print for blocks, third border, and single-fold binding
- ⅔ yard *total* of assorted green prints for blocks
- 2 yards of tan paisley for fourth border
- 4 yards of fabric for backing
- 73" × 73" square of batting

Cutting

All measurements include ¼" seam allowances.

From the cream print, cut *along the lengthwise grain*:
2 strips, 1½" × 52½"
2 strips, 1½" × 50½"

From the remainder of the cream print, cut:
32 squares, 5⅜" × 5⅜"; cut in half diagonally to yield 64 large triangles
32 squares, 5" × 5"
48 squares, 3⅜" × 3⅜"; cut into quarters diagonally to yield 192 small triangles

From the red floral, cut *along the lengthwise grain*:
2 strips, 1½" × 50½"
2 strips, 1½" × 48½"

From the assorted red prints and remainder of the red floral, cut a *total* of:
32 squares, 5" × 5"
48 squares, 3⅜" × 3⅜"; cut into quarters diagonally to yield 192 small triangles

From the green sprig print, cut:
7 strips, 1⅛" × 42"

Continued on page 73

*By **Jo Morton**; machine quilted by **Maggi Honeyman***

Continued from page 71

From the remaining green sprig print, cut *along the lengthwise grain*:

2 strips, 1½" × 54½"
2 strips, 1½" × 52½"

From the assorted green prints and remainder of the green sprig print, cut a *total* of:

32 squares, 5⅜" × 5⅜"; cut in half diagonally to yield 96 large triangles

From the tan paisley, cut *along the lengthwise grain*:

2 strips, 6½" × 66½"
2 strips, 6½" × 54½"

Making the Blocks

Use a scant ¼" seam allowance. Press all seam allowances as shown by the arrows in the illustrations.

1 Draw a diagonal line from corner to corner in both directions on the wrong side of each cream 5" square, creating an X.

2 Layer a marked square right sides together with a red 5" square. Sew a scant ¼" from both sides of the drawn lines. Cut the layered squares in half horizontally and vertically first, and then cut the individual units apart on the marked lines to make eight half-square-triangle units. Trim each unit to measure 2" square. Repeat to make a total of 256 units.

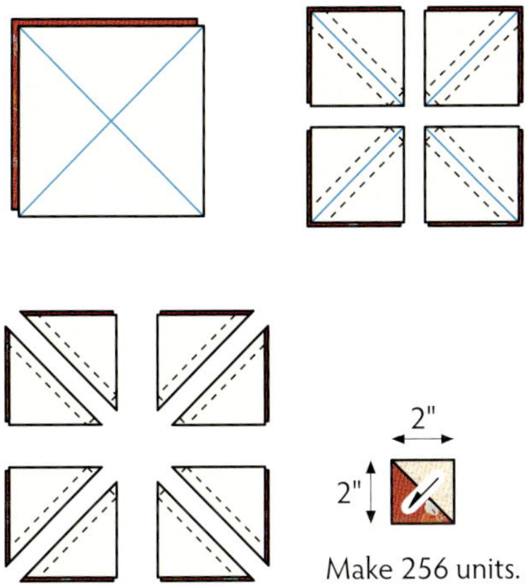

Make 256 units.

3 Arrange four half-square-triangle units, three red small triangles, and three cream small triangles in four vertical rows. Sew the pieces in each row together. Pin and sew the units together, matching seam intersections. Refer to "Clipping Trick" on page 92 to clip the seam intersections. Press the clipped intersections open. Repeat to make a total of 64 center units.

Make 64.

4 Sew a large cream triangle to the red edge of a unit from step 3 and a large green triangle to the cream edge. The block should measure 6½" square, including seam allowances. Repeat to make a total of 64 blocks.

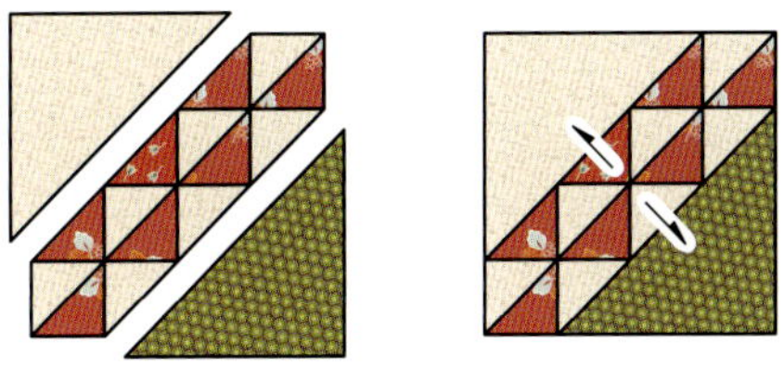

Make 64 blocks, 6½" × 6½".

Assembling the Quilt Top

1 Refer to the quilt assembly diagram below to arrange the blocks into eight rows of eight blocks each, rotating the blocks to form the pattern. When you're satisfied with the arrangement, separate the rows in half vertically and horizontally so you have four quadrants of consisting of four rows of four blocks each. Sew together the blocks in each row of each quadrant. Pin and join the rows in each quadrant, matching seam intersections. Clip the seam intersections. Press the seam allowances toward the green print and press the clipped intersections open.

2 Pin and sew the quadrants into two halves, matching seam intersections. Clip the seam intersections. Press the seam allowances toward the green print and press the clipped intersections open. Join the halves to complete the quilt center, continuing to clip seam intersections and press toward the green print. The quilt top should measure 48½" square, including seam allowances.

3 Refer to the adding borders diagram on page 75 to pin and sew the red 1½" × 48½" border strips to the top and bottom of the quilt. Pin and sew the red 1½" × 50½" border strips to the sides of the quilt. Repeat with the cream and then the green 1½"-wide border strips, sewing the shorter strips to the top and bottom first and then adding the longer strips to the sides. The quilt top should measure 54½" square, including seam allowances.

Quilt assembly

4 Pin and sew the paisley 6½" × 54½" border strips to the top and bottom of the quilt. Pin and sew the paisley 6½" × 66½" border strips to the sides of the quilt. The quilt top should measure 66½" square.

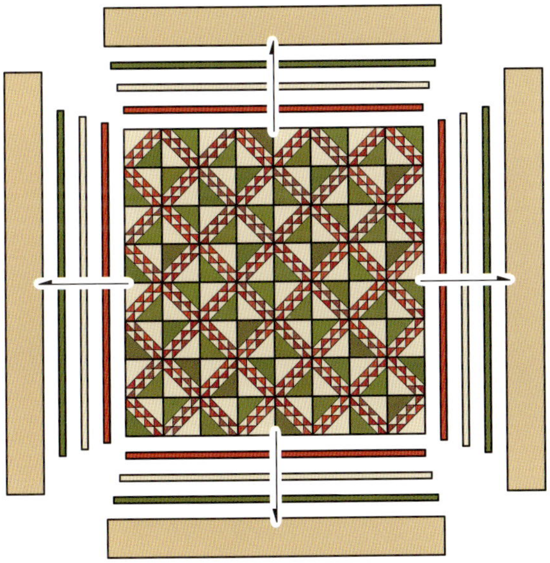

Adding borders

Quilting and Finishing

For more information about any finishing steps, visit ShopMartingale.com/HowtoQuilt.

1 Layer the quilt top, batting, and backing. Baste the layers together.

2 Hand or machine quilt as desired. The quilt shown is machine quilted with a square feathered wreath in each of the Hourglass blocks that are formed by the two large green and cream triangles. The half-square-triangle units are stitched with a continuous line in thread colors to match the triangles. The red and green borders are quilted with a loopy design, and the cream border features a curvy line down the center. A feather design is quilted in the outer paisley border.

3 Use the green 1⅛"-wide strips to make single-fold binding; attach the binding to the quilt. For more detailed information about my technique for making the binding and attaching it, see “Single-Fold Binding” on page 94.

Effie's Baskets

Five antique blocks that I purchased several years ago in Houston became the inspiration for this quilt. I made it for the annual Boxwood and Berries event at the Country Sampler shop in Spring Green, Wisconsin. It started as an all-brown quilt, but as usual, I sneaked in a little rusty red to make me happy. The brown toile and ticking stripe really set off the blocks, don't you think?

Finished Quilt: 57⅞" × 68⅞"   **Finished Block:** 6¼" × 6¼"

Materials

Yardage is based on 42"-wide fabric. Fat quarters are 18" × 21".

- 2⅝ yards *total* of assorted medium and dark prints for baskets
- 2⅔ yards *total* of assorted shirting prints for block backgrounds and corner setting triangles
- 1⅓ yards of brown printed (not woven) ticking stripe for sashing strips and single-fold binding
- 1 fat quarter of rust-and-gold plaid for sashing cornerstones
- 1¾ yards of brown print for inner border
- 1⅞ yards of brown bird toile for outer border
- 3½ yards of fabric for backing
- 64" × 75" piece of batting

Cutting

All measurements include ¼" seam allowances. For each full and half block, choose one shirting print for the background and one medium and one dark print for the basket and handle.

Cutting for 1 Full Block

You'll need a total of 32 blocks, but it's easier to cut one at a time.

From either the medium or dark print for basket and handle, cut:

1 square, 5⅞" × 5⅞"; cut in half diagonally to make 2 large triangles (1 is extra)*

3 squares, 2⅛" × 2⅛"; cut in half diagonally to make 6 small triangles

2 squares, 1¾" × 1¾"

From the other medium or dark print for basket, cut:

4 squares, 1¾" × 1¾"

From the shirting print, cut:

1 square, 5⅞" × 5⅞"; cut in half diagonally to yield 2 large triangles (1 is extra)

1 square, 3½" × 3½"; cut in half diagonally to yield 2 medium triangles (1 is extra)

2 rectangles, 1¾" × 4¼"

**One square is enough to make the handles for two blocks, so if you use the same fabric for the handle of two blocks, you'll only need to cut one square.*

Continued on page 78

Continued from page 77

Cutting for 1 Half Block

You'll need a total of 14 half blocks, but it's easier to cut one at a time.

From either the medium or dark print, cut:

- 1 square, 2⅛" × 2⅛"; cut in half diagonally to yield 2 small triangles
- 2 squares, 1¾" × 1¾"

From the other medium or dark print, cut:

- 2 squares, 2⅛" × 2⅛"; cut in half diagonally to yield 4 small triangles (1 is extra)
- 1 square, 1¾" × 1¾"

From the shirting print, cut:

- 1 square, 3½" × 3½"; cut in half diagonally to yield 2 medium triangles (1 is extra)
- 2 rectangles, 1¾" × 4¼"

Cutting for Sashing, Setting, Borders, and Binding

From the brown ticking stripe, cut:

- 16 strips, 2" × 42"; crosscut into 80 strips, 2" × 6¾"
- 7 strips, 1⅛" × 42"

From the rust-and-gold plaid, fussy cut:
49 identical squares, 2" × 2"

From the assorted shirting prints, cut a *total* of:

- 2 squares, 6" × 6"; cut in half diagonally to yield 4 corner triangles

From the brown print, cut *along the lengthwise grain*:

- 2 strips, 1¼" × 56⅞"
- 2 strips, 1¼" × 44⅜"

From the brown bird toile, cut *along the lengthwise grain*:

- 2 strips, 6½" × 57⅞"
- 2 strips, 6½" × 56⅞"

Making the Full Basket Blocks

Use a scant ¼" seam allowance. Press all seam allowances as shown by the arrows in the illustrations.

1 Select one set of full Basket block pieces. Using the pattern on page 83 and the large medium or dark triangle, prepare a basket handle using your favorite appliqué method. Appliqué the handle to the large shirting triangle.

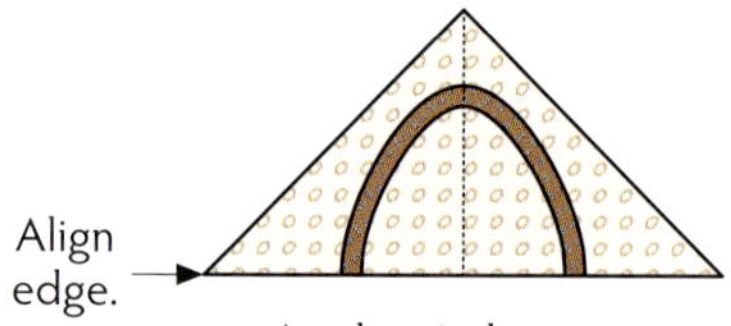

Appliqué placement

2 Sew a small dark or medium triangle to one end of each shirting rectangle as shown to make the basket-feet units.

Make 1 unit.

Make 1 unit.

3 Arrange the remaining dark and medium pieces into four rows as shown on page 80. Sew the pieces in each row together. Pin and sew the rows together, matching seam intersections, to make the basket unit. Refer to "Clipping Trick"

*By **Jo Morton**; machine quilted by **Lori Kukuk***

on page 92 to clip the seam intersections. Press the seam allowances toward the dark pieces and press the clipped intersections open.

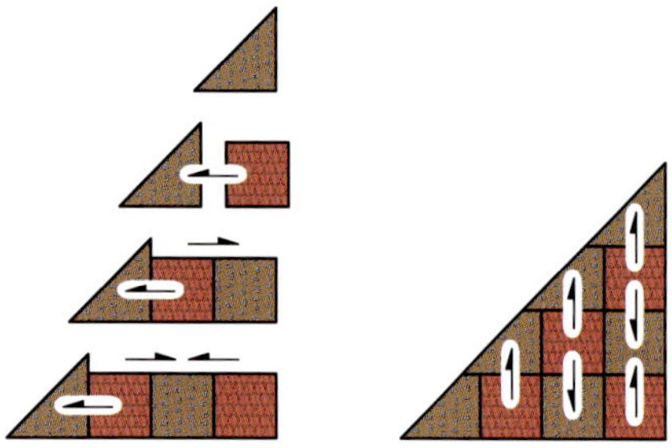

Make 1 unit.

4 Sew the basket-feet units from step 2 to the short sides of the basket unit, matching seam intersections. Add the appliquéd handle triangle from step 1 to the long edge of the basket unit. Center the shirting medium triangle along the feet edge of the basket unit and sew it in place. Trim the block to measure 6¾" square.

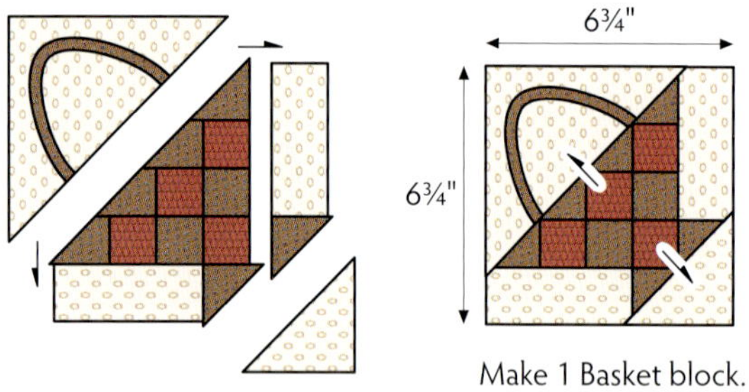

Make 1 Basket block.

5 Repeat steps 1–4 to make a total of 32 full Basket blocks.

Making the Half Basket Blocks

1 Select one set of Half Basket block pieces. Sew a small dark or medium triangle to one end of each shirting rectangle as shown to make the basket-feet units.

Make 1 unit.

Make 1 unit.

2 Arrange the remaining dark and medium pieces into three rows as shown. Sew the pieces in each row together. Pin and sew the rows together, matching seam intersections, to make the basket unit. Clip the seam intersections. Press the seam allowances toward the dark pieces and press the clipped intersections open.

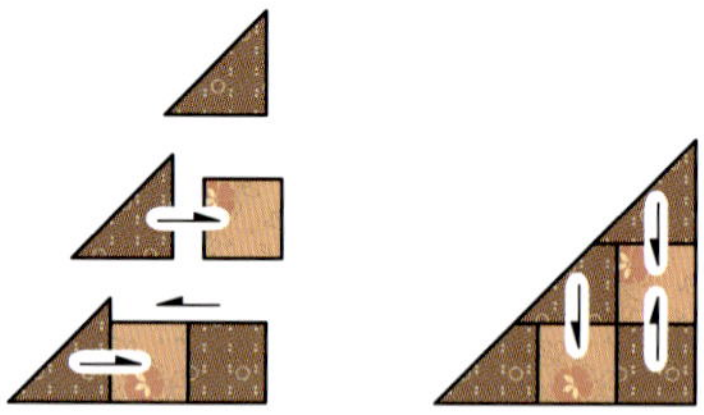

Make 1 unit.

3 Sew the basket-feet units from step 1 to the short sides of the basket unit, matching seam intersections. Center the shirting medium triangle along the feet edge of the basket unit and sew it in place. Trim the rectangle ends even with the upper edge of the basket unit.

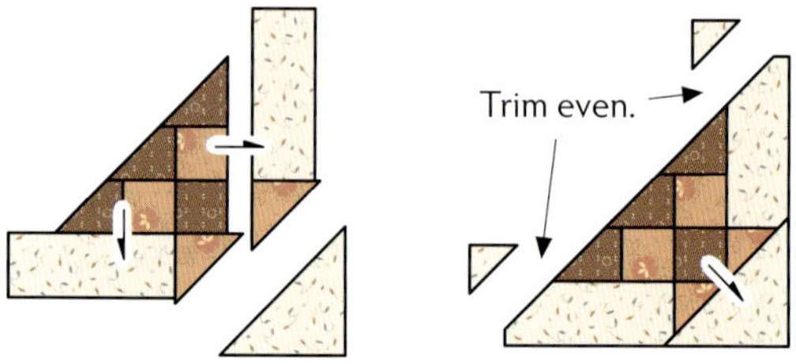

Make 1 Half Basket block.

4 Repeat steps 1–3 to make a total of 14 Half Basket blocks.

Assembling the Quilt Top

1 Refer to the quilt assembly diagram below to arrange the full Basket blocks, the ticking 2" × 6¾" sashing strips, and the rust-and-gold 2" sashing cornerstones in 17 diagonal rows. Add the Half Basket blocks to the edges and the shirting corner triangles to the layout. Note that the cornerstones along the edges will be trimmed when squaring up the quilt center before adding the inner border.

2 Sew the full blocks, half blocks, and sashing strips in each diagonal block row together. Sew the sashing strips and cornerstones in each sashing row together.

3 Pin and sew the block rows and sashing rows together, matching seam intersections. Clip the seam intersections. Press the seam allowances toward the sashing strips and press the clipped intersections open. Add the corner triangles last.

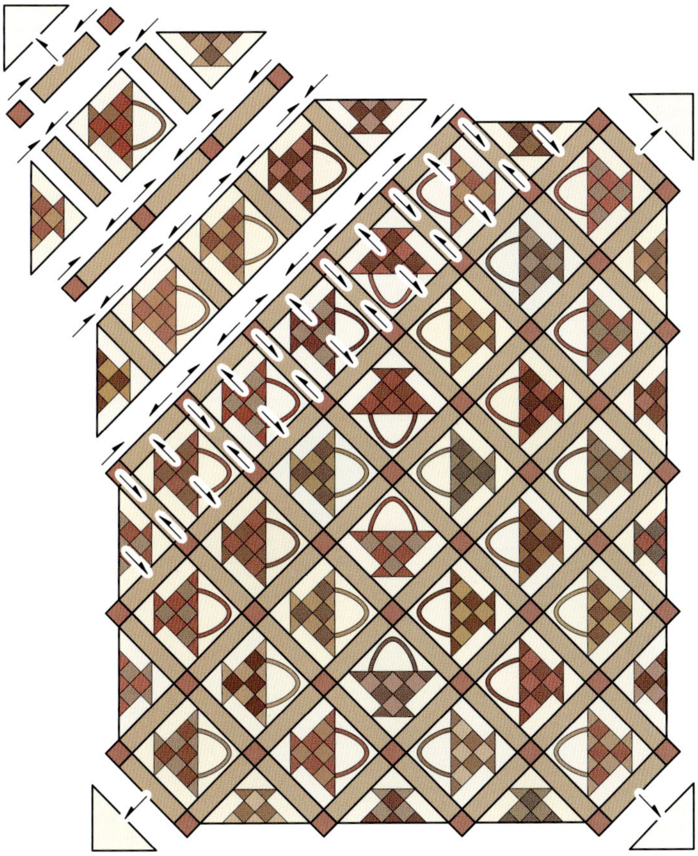

Quilt assembly

4 Trim the edges of the quilt ¼" from the inside corners of the sashing cornerstones so they're even with the edges of the Half Basket blocks. The quilt top should measure 44⅜" × 55⅜", including seam allowances.

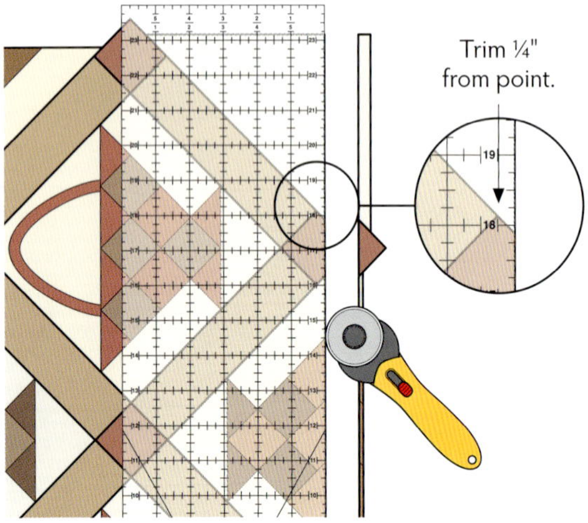

5 Pin and sew the brown 1¼" × 44⅜" inner-border strips to the top and bottom of the quilt. Pin and sew the brown 1¼" × 56⅞" inner-border strips to the sides of the quilt. The quilt top should measure 45⅞" × 56⅞", including seam allowances.

6 Pin and sew the toile 6½" × 56⅞" outer-border strips to the sides of the quilt. Pin and sew the toile 6½" × 57⅞" outer-border strips to the top and bottom of the quilt. The quilt top should measure 57⅞" × 68⅞".

Adding borders

Quilting and Finishing

For more information about any finishing steps, visit ShopMartingale.com/HowtoQuilt.

1 Layer the quilt top, batting, and backing. Baste the layers together.

2 Hand or machine quilt as desired. The quilt shown is machine quilted in the ditch along the block edges, and the blocks are quilted with a grid that forms an X. Echo quilting is featured inside and outside the block handle, with lines spaced ¼" to ⅜" apart. Parallel lines with the same spacing are quilted in the bottom triangle and in the background rectangles of each block. The sashing strips feature two arcs that intersect to form the design. The inner border is stitched in the ditch along both sides, and the outer border is quilted with a crosshatch design.

3 Use the brown ticking stripe 1⅛"-wide strips to make single-fold binding; attach the binding to the quilt. For more detailed information about my technique for making the binding and attaching it, see "Single-Fold Binding" on page 94.

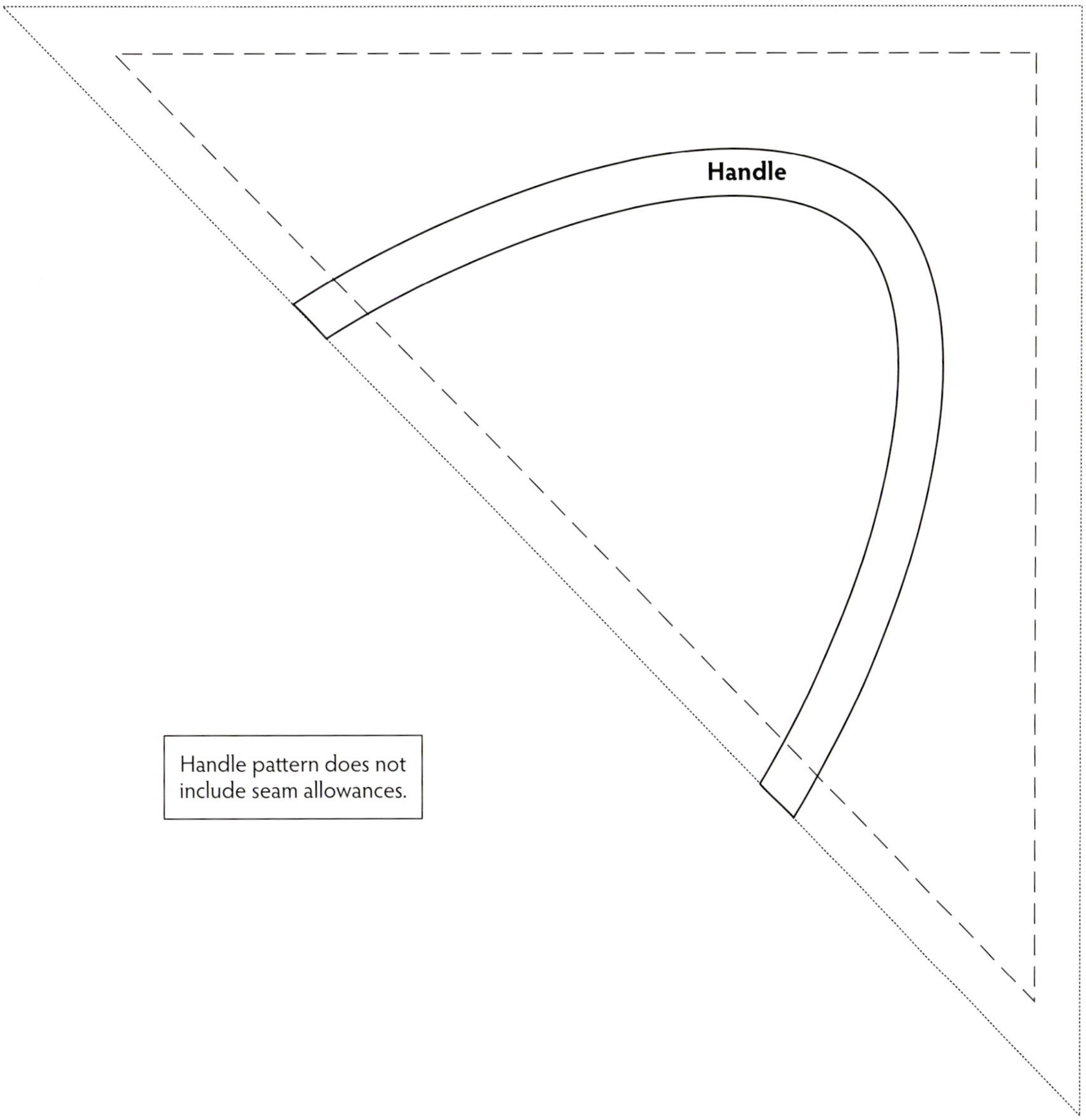

Log Cabin

Warm colors warm my heart, and the rich browns, reds, and blues in this quilt don't disappoint. Of course, I love traditional blocks too, and nothing's more traditional than a Log Cabin block. The on-point setting isn't one you're likely to see in an old quilt, but I found it much more interesting than some of the straight settings I was playing with. I hope you like it too!

Finished Quilt: 31½" × 38¼" **Finished Block:** 4¾" × 4¾"

Materials

Yardage is based on 42"-wide fabric.

- ⅛ yard of brick red print #1 for block center squares
- ⅓ yard *total* of assorted light prints for blocks
- ⅓ yard *total* of assorted blue prints for blocks
- ½ yard *total* of assorted brown prints for blocks
- ⅜ yard *total* of assorted dark blue prints for blocks
- ½ yard *total* of assorted brick red prints for blocks
- ⅜ yard *total* of assorted dark brown prints for blocks
- ⅓ yard of cream print for setting triangles
- 1 yard of brick red print #2 for inner border
- ½ yard of blue dotted stripe for outer border
- ¼ yard of dark brown print for single-fold binding
- 1¼ yards of fabric for backing
- 38" × 45" piece of batting

Cutting

All measurements include ¼" seam allowances. For this quilt, you need 12 blue blocks and 12 brown blocks. Choose four prints for the logs of each block. Because brick red print #1 is used for the center square of each block, cutting instructions also include the total number of pieces if you want to cut them all at once.

Cutting for 1 Blue Block

You'll need a total of 12 blocks, but it's easier to cut them one at a time. For the light half of each blue block, use a light and a brown print. For the dark half of each blue block, use a dark blue print and a blue or brown print.

From brick red print #1, cut:
1 square (12 total), 1¼" × 1¼"

From the light print, cut ***along the lengthwise grain*****:**
1 log, 1" × 1¼" (A)
1 log, 1" × 1¾" (B)
1 log, 1" × 3¼" (I)
1 log, 1" × 3¾" (J)

Continued on page 86

Continued from page 85

From the blue print, cut *along the lengthwise grain*:
- 1 log, 1" × 1¾" (C)
- 1 log, 1" × 2¼" (D)
- 1 log, 1" × 3¾" (K)
- 1 log, 1" × 4¼" (L)

From the brown print, cut *along the lengthwise grain*:
- 1 log, 1" × 2¼" (E)
- 1 log, 1" × 2¾" (F)
- 1 log, 1" × 4¼" (M)
- 1 log, 1" × 4¾" (N)

From the dark blue print, cut *along the lengthwise grain*:
- 1 log, 1" × 2¾" (G)
- 1 log, 1" × 3¼" (H)
- 1 log, 1" × 4¾" (O)
- 1 log, 1" × 5¼" (P)

Cutting for 1 Brown Block

You'll need a total of 12 blocks, but it's easier to cut them one at a time. For the light half of each brown block, use a light print and a brick red print. For the dark half use a dark brown and a brown print.

From brick red print #1, cut:
- 1 square (12 total), 1¼" × 1¼"

From the light print, cut *along the lengthwise grain*:
- 1 log, 1" × 1¼" (A)
- 1 log, 1" × 1¾" (B)
- 1 log, 1" × 3¼" (I)
- 1 log, 1" × 3¾" (J)

From the brown print, cut *along the lengthwise grain*:
- 1 log, 1" × 1¾" (C)
- 1 log, 1" × 2¼" (D)
- 1 log, 1" × 3¾" (K)
- 1 log, 1" × 4¼" (L)

From the brick red print for blocks, cut *along the lengthwise grain*:
- 1 log, 1" × 2¼" (E)
- 1 log, 1" × 2¾" (F)
- 1 log, 1" × 4¼" (M)
- 1 log, 1" × 4¾" (N)

From the dark brown print, cut *along the lengthwise grain*:
- 1 log, 1" × 2¾" (G)
- 1 log, 1" × 3¼" (H)
- 1 log, 1" × 4¾" (O)
- 1 log, 1" × 5¼" (P)

Cutting for Setting, Borders, and Binding

From the cream print, cut:
- 3 squares, 8" × 8"; cut into quarters diagonally to yield 12 side setting triangles (2 are extra)
- 1 square, 8" × 8"; cut in half diagonally to yield 2 corner setting triangles
- 1 square, 4½" × 4½"; cut in half diagonally to yield 2 corner setting triangles

From brick red print #2, cut *along the lengthwise grain*:
- 2 strips, 1¼" × 30¾"
- 2 strips, 1¼" × 25½"
- 4 squares, 3½" × 3½"

From the blue dotted stripe, cut:
- 2 strips, 3½" × 32¼"
- 2 strips, 3½" × 25½"

From the dark brown print for binding, cut:
- 4 strips, 1⅛" × 42"

CUTTING LENGTHWISE LOGS

The blocks will turn out much flatter if you cut the logs along the lengthwise grain. The lengthwise grain has less stretch, so the logs are more stable. However, if I have a stripe or print that would be more interesting cut across the width of the fabric, I'll make an exception to my rule.

Making the Blocks

Use a scant ¼" seam allowance. Press all seam allowances as shown by the arrows in the illustrations.

1 Select one set of block pieces. Sew the light A log to the right edge of the brick red 1¼" square. Sew the light B log to the bottom edge of the square. The unit should measure 1¾" square, including seam allowances.

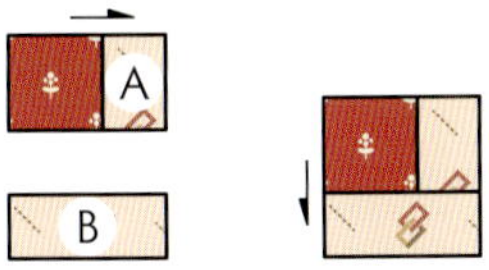

Make 1 unit, 1¾" × 1¾".

2 Sew the C log to the left edge of the square, and then sew the D log to the top of the square. You have now added one round of logs to the center square. The unit should measure 2¼" square, including seam allowances. ***Note:*** When pressing, be careful that you don't distort the unit. Measure it after adding and pressing each round to keep the block accurate. Each complete round of strips will add 1" to the width and height.

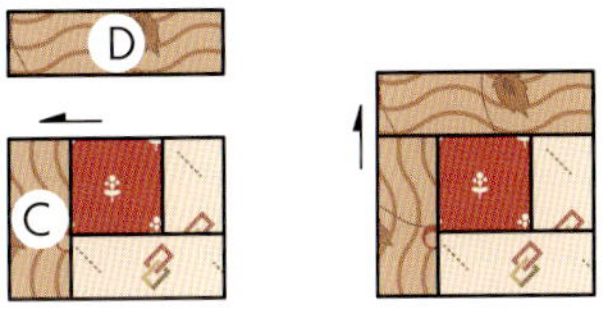

Make 1 unit, 2¼" × 2¼".

3 Continue adding strips in alphabetical order, working clockwise around the unit as shown. The block should measure 5¼" square, including seam allowances.

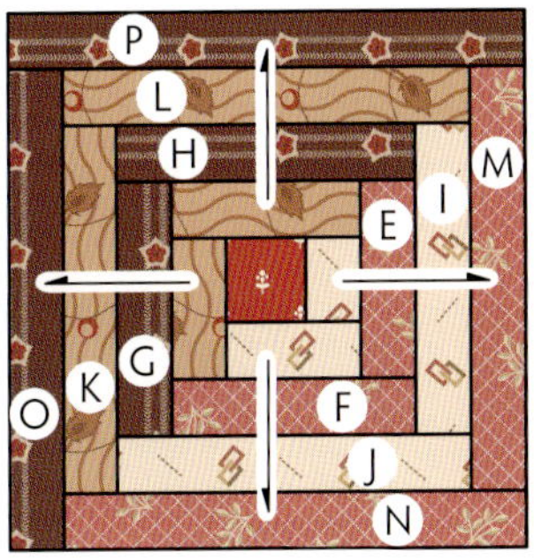

Make 1 block, 5¼" × 5¼".

4 Repeat steps 1–3 to make a total of 12 blue blocks and 12 brown blocks.

Assembling the Quilt Top

1 Referring to the quilt assembly diagram below, arrange the blocks and cream setting triangles in seven diagonal rows, alternating the blue and brown blocks in each row. Sew the pieces in each row together. Pin and sew the rows together, matching seam intersections. Refer to "Clipping Trick" on page 92 to clip the seam intersections. Press the seam allowances toward the setting triangles and the brown blocks and press the clipped intersections open. Add the corner triangles last.

2 Trim the edges of the quilt ¼" from the block points. The quilt top should measure 24" × 30¾", including seam allowances.

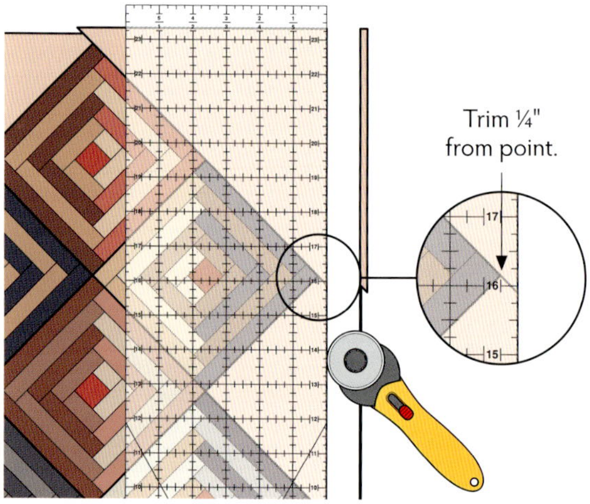

Quilt assembly

By **Jo Morton;** machine quilted by **Lori Kukuk**

3 Pin and sew the 1¼" × 30¾" brick red #2 border strips to the sides of the quilt. Pin and sew the 1¼" × 25½" brick red #2 border strips to the top and bottom of the quilt. The quilt top should measure 25½" × 32¼", including seam allowances.

STABILIZING THE BORDER STRIPS

I normally cut border strips along the lengthwise grain, for exactly the same reason I suggested cutting the block logs that way—they're more stable. The outer-border striped fabric was printed in such a way that I couldn't do that and get the effect I wanted, so I had to cut the strips from selvage to selvage. To stabilize the strips and keep them from stretching, I stay stitched the outer edge of each strip before sewing it to the quilt top.

4 Pin and sew the blue dotted stripe 3½" × 32¼" outer-border strips to the sides of the quilt. Sew the 3½" brick red print #2 squares to the ends of the blue dotted stripe 3½" × 25½" strips. Pin and sew these strips to the top and bottom of the quilt. The quilt top should measure 31½" × 38¼".

Adding borders

Quilting and Finishing

For more information about any finishing steps, visit ShopMartingale.com/HowtoQuilt.

1 Layer the quilt top, batting, and backing. Baste the layers together.

2 Hand or machine quilt as desired. The quilt shown is machine stitched in the ditch of each block seam. The setting triangles are quilted with a crosshatch design, and a straight line is quilted through the center of the inner border. Each border corner square features an eight-petal flower, and the remainder of the border is stitched with a piano-key design.

3 Use the dark brown 1⅛"-wide strips to make single-fold binding; attach the binding to the quilt. For more detailed information about my technique for making the binding and attaching it, see "Single-Fold Binding" on page 94.

Jo's Favorite Techniques

For the quilts in this book, you'll need basic rotary-cutting and machine-piecing skills. If you need assistance with either of those, I recommend you go to ShopMartingale.com/HowtoQuilt for free downloadable information. Here, I'll cover some of the specific materials and techniques that I use.

Prewashing Fabric

I prewash all my fabrics, for several reasons. I prefer the way prewashed fabric handles during the process of piecing or appliquéing. The fabric weave tightens up during the washing and drying process, which not only makes it easier to handle but also makes it less likely to ravel. Prewashing also gets rid of any chemicals used in the finishing process. I generally don't work with precut fabrics; if you do, you may not want to prewash those.

I wash the fabric with my regular laundry soap, using the gentle wash cycle and cold water. I run it through the entire cycle and then place it in the dryer on the permanent press setting until it's almost dry. Don't overdry the fabric, or you'll set in wrinkles. After I take it out of the dryer, I fold it immediately and place it on the shelf. I press the fabric when I'm ready to cut it for a project.

Accurate Sewing and Piecing

Accuracy is important to ensure that blocks will go together nicely. It starts with accurate cutting and continues with accurate piecing. There are several factors to consider.

Start by using a *scant* ¼" seam allowance. Why scant? When you press the seam allowances, the fold of the fabric takes up part of the seam and creates a small amount of "shrinkage." The more seams you have, the more shrinkage occurs. By sewing one or two threads less than an exact ¼", you can compensate for the fold. So let *scant* be your friend!

Thread can also create added bulk in the seam allowance. A finer weight will create less bulk for flatter, more accurate seams. I prefer 50-weight, 100% cotton DMC thread, which is a high-quality thread for hand or machine piecing.

I machine piece my blocks with one of my Pfaff sewing machines. All of these machines have a dual-feed mechanism, and I engage it to keep my seams straight and keep the fabric layers from shifting.

Clipping Trick

At the intersection of the seams, clip into the seam allowance almost to the stitching on each side, ¼" from the seam (the clips will be ½" apart). The clips should be lined up with the outside edge of the seam allowance. Press the seam allowances open between the clips.

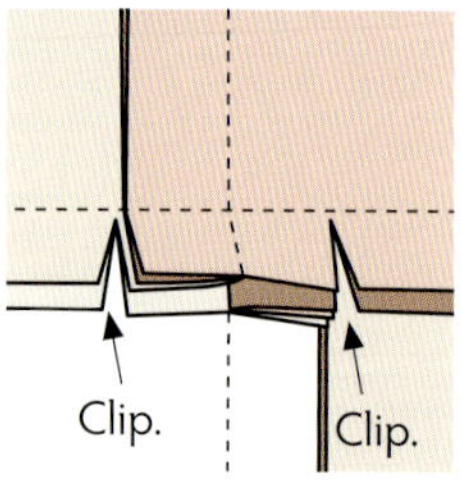

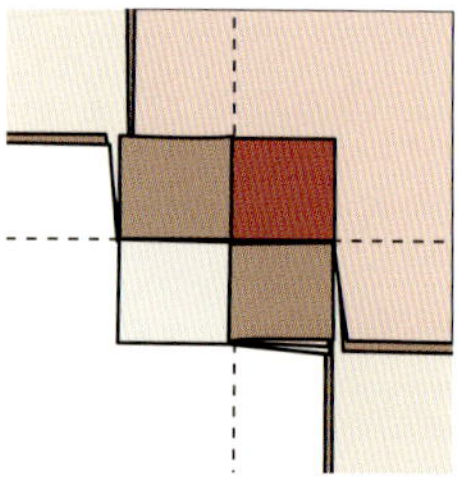

Cutting Borders

I recommend cutting borders along the lengthwise grain of the fabric, parallel to the selvage. This has the least amount of stretch and will give the quilt nice straight edges. I seldom recommend cutting borders from selvage to selvage, due to the stretch in the fabric.

There are always exceptions to this rule, however, such as when using a stripe cut crosswise for effect. If you do cut crosswise, I would suggest stay stitching to prevent the outer edges from stretching.

Back-Basting Needle-Turn Appliqué

Two benefits of this technique are that the pieces will be correctly positioned and the appliqués will lie flatter. Be sure to read through the instructions first to get an understanding of the technique; then come back and begin.

What You'll Need

Marking tools. Use a marking pen (I use Clover, fine white, item #517) or a mechanical pencil (I use .7 or .9 mm lead) to trace the appliqué shape.

Scissors. Use a sharp pair of fabric scissors (my favorite is Dovo brand with either a 5" blade or the Dovo 4" embroidery scissors) to trim away the excess fabric, leaving a generous ⅛" seam allowance.

Needles and thread. For back-basting, use a light color of quilting thread. For appliquéing the shapes, use a 50- or 60-weight, 3-ply thread that matches or blends with the appliqués. For needles, I like Jeana Kimball size 9 and 11 straw needles used with a Clover needle threader. I recommend the Clover Double Needle Threader (item #462/ NV).

Light box. Use a light box to trace the appliqué shapes onto the background. A light box is optional but very helpful.

How to Appliqué

1 Cut out the background piece at least 1" larger than the finished measurements.

2 Use the appliqué patterns and the placement guide to create a full-sized pattern. Place the pattern on a light box or other light source, with the reversed (or unmarked) side facing up. Place the background piece, wrong side up, on top of the pattern. If you can't see the pattern through the fabric, remove the fabric and use a black permanent pen to trace the shape on the wrong side of the paper.

3 Use a mechanical pencil to trace the shape onto the wrong side of the background fabric. Determine the appliqué stitching sequence. As with any other appliqué method, stitch the shapes that go under other pieces first.

4 From the appropriate appliqué fabric, cut a piece that is large enough to cover the entire appliqué shape, with enough extra for seam allowance. Place the appliqué piece on the background fabric, right side facing up, on top of the traced shape. Hold the background fabric up to the light so you can make sure the correct area is covered. Pin the appliqué piece in place.

5 Thread a size 9 straw needle with a length of thread, but don't knot the thread. Using a short running stitch (9 to 10 stitches per inch), and working from the wrong side, baste the appliqué fabric to the background, stitching directly on the marked line of the shape. Start on a straight edge and leave a 2" thread tail at the beginning and end or anytime you start and end with a new thread.

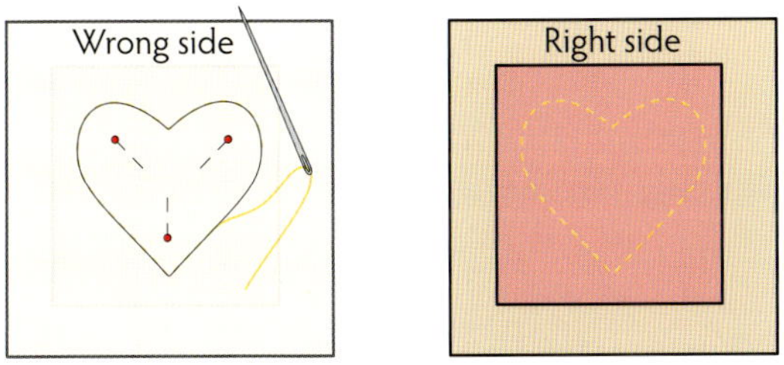

Baste with small running stitches exactly on drawn line.

Note: Don't be misled by the word *basting*. Basting means to temporarily secure two fabrics together. While this is often done with a long running stitch, the stitch length does not define the term, and in this case it's necessary to use a shorter stitch length. The combination of the large needle and heavy quilting thread perforates the fabric to create a memory line for turning under the fabric.

6 Turn the pieces over to the right side. Use sharp scissors to cut away the excess appliqué fabric, leaving a generous ⅛" seam allowance.

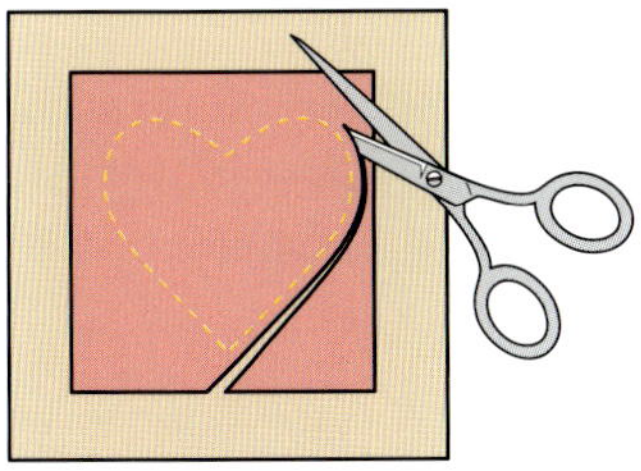

LET IT REST

I recommend basting one evening, letting the piece sit overnight, and then proceeding with the appliqué process the following evening. This gives time for the perforation to set. You won't see the perforation when you stitch, but the appliqué will turn under nicely along the perforated edge created by the basting.

7 Thread a size 11 straw needle with an 18" length of 50- or 60-weight thread to match or blend with the appliqué fabric. Knot one end of the thread. You'll be working with a single strand. Starting at a basting-thread tail, always on a straight edge, use the threaded sewing needle to pull the basting thread to the top, and then pull out two or three basting stitches.

8 Holding the fabrics in place with your left (or nonsewing) hand, insert the needle into the basting line from the wrong side of the appliqué fabric. This will hide the knot between the appliqué fabric and background fabric (I don't leave knots on the back). Use the needle to turn under about ½" of the seam allowance along the previously basted line.

9 Insert the needle into the background as close to where the thread came out of the fold as possible. Take a stitch about 1/16" wide, coming up through the folded edge of the appliqué. Barely catch the folded edge of the appliqué so the thread will not be seen.

10 After a few stitches, use the needle to remove a few more basting stitches. Continue stitching around the entire shape in this manner.

How to Stitch Inner Points

1 When you come to an inside point and can't turn under the fabric any more, use sharp embroidery scissors and carefully clip *to* the point. Use your needle to turn under the fabric toward the inside point. Take smaller stitches to the point.

2 When you reach the point, turn under the seam allowance on the other side, carefully smoothing it with a needle. Making sure all threads are turned under, take an extra stitch in the inside point. Continue up the other side, gradually increasing stitch length from 1⁄16" to 1⁄8".

How to Stitch Outer Points

1 For a sharp point, stitch to the point, fold under the end at a 90° angle, and take one stitch to secure the fold. Then use your needle to turn under the other side, sweeping the fabric under with your needle. You may need to carefully trim away excess fabric *at* the point when turning, since excess fabric can cause a rounded point and a lump.

2 Give the thread a tug to pull out the point, hold the turned-under fabric down with your thumb, and continue with the appliqué stitch.

MARK THE POINTS

At inner and outer points, I use a Clover white marking pen to mark over the basting thread on the right side of fabric. When the thread is removed, I follow the line to know how far to stitch and clip. The white line disappears when using an iron or with water. Always follow the manufacturer's instructions before using the pen.

Ending Off

1 After stitching the shape in place, insert the needle next to the appliqué edge and pull the thread through to the back.

2 Wrap the thread around the needle twice, hold the needle down next to the fabric, and pull the needle and thread through to create a knot just on top of the fabric.

3 Insert your needle where the thread came out; pull to bury the knot between the background fabric and the appliqué fabric. ***Note:*** I don't cut away any of the background fabric behind the appliqués; the antique quilts I have examined had backgrounds that were left intact.

Batting

I use 100% cotton batting for my quilts because it contributes to the flat, antique look and feel that I prefer. Mountain Mist Blue Ribbon cotton batting has been my favorite for years. It needles wonderfully for hand quilting and is equally wonderful for machine quilting to achieve a vintage appearance. Cotton batting drapes nicely and washes beautifully! I try other battings from time to time and always return to Mountain Mist Blue Ribbon.

Single-Fold Binding

I use single-fold binding on all my quilts. I find single-fold binding on most nineteenth-century quilts. If it was good enough for them, it's good enough for me. To prevent the binding from stretching, I recommend using a walking foot or engaging the machine's dual-feed mechanism.

1 Cut the number of 1⅛"-wide strips necessary to go around the quilt, adding 10" extra for seaming. Cut the strips crosswise (across the width of the fabric, from selvage to selvage). Using a diagonal seam, join the short ends, right sides together, to make one long piece. Press seam allowances open.

2 With right sides together, align a raw edge of the binding with the raw edge of the quilt. Beginning about 5" to 6" from the binding end, sew the binding to the quilt using a ¼" seam allowance. Stop sewing ¼" from the corner; backstitch and remove the quilt from the machine.

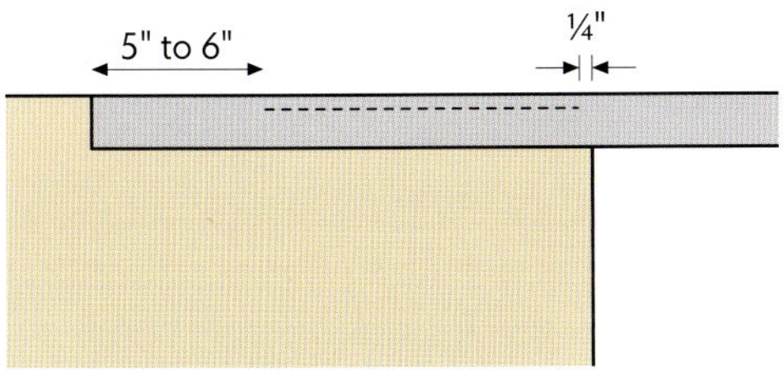

3 Rotate the quilt a quarter turn to be ready to sew the next side. Fold up the binding at a 90° angle.

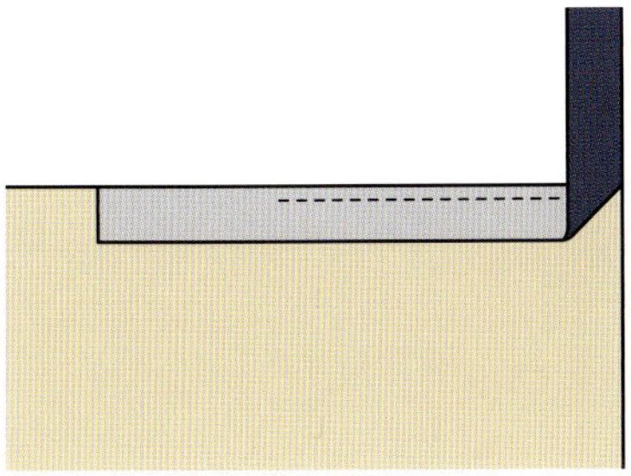

4 Fold the binding back down over the first fold and align the binding raw edge with the quilt raw edge. Reposition the quilt under the presser foot. Beginning with a backstitch, continue sewing the binding to the quilt top. Sew until you are ¼" from the next corner; backstitch. Repeat the folding and stitching steps at each corner.

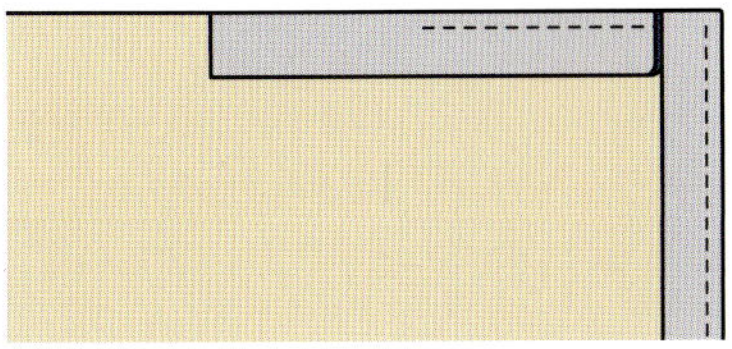

5 Stop sewing about 8" to 10" from the start. Remove the quilt from the machine.

6 Fold the beginning of the binding strip toward the center of the quilt at a 90° angle. Repeat, folding the end of the binding strip toward the edge of the quilt at a 90° angle, leaving about a ⅛" gap between the folds. Press. By leaving the gap, you ensure that the binding will lie nice and flat.

7 Align the fold lines, right sides together, and pin them in place. Sew on the fold line, backstitching at the beginning and end. Trim the excess binding strip, leaving a ¼" seam allowance. Press the seam allowances open. Finish sewing the binding in place.

8 Trim the batting and backing even with the quilt edges. Fold the binding away from the quilt and turn the raw edge under ¼". Fold the binding over the quilt edge and pin it in place so it covers the first stitches, mitering corners as you go.

9 Blindstitch the binding to the quilt back, using small, closely spaced stitches and being careful not to stitch through to the front of the quilt. I recommend taking three or four extra stitches on the folds of the mitered corners to hold them in place.

About the Author

Jo Morton is a quiltmaker, fabric designer, teacher, author, and lecturer. Her use of color and design, as well as her fine stitchery, give her quilts the feeling of being made in the nineteenth century. Using an antique quilt as a source of inspiration, she creates an interpretation. Her quilts complement both country and contemporary settings, and her work is included in private and public collections across the country.

In 1980 Jo took her first quilting class, and in 1985 she created her first "made to look old" quilt. She determined early on that if she ever hoped to make all the quilts she wanted to make, they would have to be small, and this size works perfectly in the small 1929 bungalow where she lives.

Jo is known for her "Jo's Little Women Club" patterns, available through participating quilt shops since 2003. Her quilts have appeared in numerous magazines, and she's made several television appearances.

Jo lives in Nebraska City with her husband, Russ. Follow Jo on Instagram @joquilts.